The Heart of Prayer

Brother Ramon studied Theology at Cardiff,
Zurich and Edinburgh and is a member of
the Anglican Society of St Francis. He was
guardian of Glasshampton Monastery until
his departure to explore the hermit life.

Also by the same author,
available from Marshall Pickering

FORTY DAYS AND FORTY NIGHTS
HEAVEN ON EARTH
A HIDDEN FIRE
THE WAY OF LOVE

The Heart of Prayer

Finding a time, a place and a way to pray

BROTHER RAMON SSF

Illustrations by Molly Dowell

Marshall Pickering
An Imprint of HarperCollinsPublishers

Marshall Pickering is an Imprint of
HarperCollins*Religious*
Part of HarperCollins*Publishers*
77–85 Fulham Palace Road, London W6 8JB

First published in Great Britain
in 1995 by Marshall Pickering

1 3 5 7 9 10 8 6 4 2

A catalogue record for this book is
available from the British Library

0551 02907–2

Scripture quotations are from the New Revised Standard
Version of the Bible, copyright 1989 by the Division of
Christian Education of the National Council of the
Churches of Christ in the USA.

Cover Photograph of the author by Molly Dowell

Printed and bound in Great Britain by
HarperCollinsManufacturing Glasgow

Contents

PART III: PASTORAL REFLECTIONS

Preface

COME WITH ME

The Kyoto stepping stones on the cover of this book symbolize the precarious and wonderful journey to God which calls us all, and I reflect upon it in these opening words.

Twenty years ago the realization really hit me — that perhaps I was called towards an exploration of the hermit life;
Ten years ago I moved from an exceptionally busy month's Franciscan mission in the Welsh diocese of Swansea and Brecon straight into six months' solitude in a stone cottage opposite the island of Bardsey off the coast of North Wales;
Today I am well into my fifth year of hermit exploration.

All the promises and hopes of wonder and joy are being fulfilled, and the increasing awareness of human sorrow and lostness are part of the journey. In short, I am tasting the sweet and bitter experience of being human — for myself and for others. And all this is in the context of my search and fulfilment in God.

It is true that we cannot search for God unless we have already been found by him, and it is out of this exciting experience of prevenient grace (God leading the way) that I write to invite you to share my life for our common good.

My friend Michael took up this invitation two days ago, and

the truth was clear to us both — that I am where I am for his sake, and he is where he is for my sake. He is an enthusiastic ecumenical Christian, a priest, husband, father, and he serves as Director of the Anglican Renewal Ministries (ARM), with a charismatic and catholic ministry that incites in me a godly jealousy! And I represent for him a gospel life of solitude, simplicity and contemplative prayer for which he yearns.

He came to share with me, and went from this place blessed, refreshed and encouraged. So you are invited to share with me in this book some of the fruits of solitude and prayer, that you also may return refreshed and encouraged in spirit, to love and serve God in the place he has set you.

Part One opens up the pattern of my own pilgrimage, and though my life story may be so different from yours, the experiences will enable you to see your own humanity more clearly.

Part Two consists of a series of chapters in which you can experiment with practical ways of praying, bringing body, mind, and spirit together. The springs of spiritual creativity may well bubble up anew as you find new ways of praying and loving God, using spiritual muscles you never knew you had.

The *final section* is made up of pastoral counsel ensuring that your spirituality is not something ethereal which compartmentalizes your religious life from daily experience. Spirituality must be human, earthed in everyday experience, yet suffused with the healing power and joy of God.

Molly Dowell and I put our heads together so that she could illustrate the places around Glasshampton, and the experiences spelled out in the writing. Come with me, then, and let us share together the good things the Holy Spirit has in store for us.

Brother Ramon SSF

INTRODUCTION

Glasshampton Monastery

Personal Pilgrimage

CHILDHOOD MYSTERY

From early childhood, religious experience has been woven into my life's journey, long before I was able to describe it in words. And I don't have to label it specifically religious, though some of it is certainly that. Rather, in everything that moves me at any depth, whether in nature or in grace, I feel the reverberations of that immense mystery that has haunted me from my earliest days. And that mystery I call God.

I suppose one is expected to qualify that, and say that it is only in *positive* things I feel this mystery – things true, good and beautiful, the loveliness of nature, art, poetry, creativity and aesthetic exhilaration. But that would not be true. My sensitivity to a world of hatred, violence, hunger, cruelty and torture is sharpened and sanctified by what I can only call the divine sadness. Tears and groaning are equally a part of my experience as are ecstasy and joy. Its roots are in childhood. Words of Angelus Selesius come to mind:

Because the Godhead was
In childhood shown to me,
To Godhead and to childhood
I am drawn equally.

2

That seems to be increasingly true for me. If I want to learn more, to increase my awareness of the divine presence – I reach back in spirit to my childhood – not only to the images and experiences that were part of my infancy and boyhood, but to the perspective of innocence and wonder, mingled with expectation that often invaded my being when I was alone.

And this is no mere journey into infantile subjectivity. The more I allow my childhood dreams and experiences to flow into my present meditative life, the more I realize the 'givenness' of such experience. It is possible to read back into childhood an orderly emergence of ideas which can be clothed with the thought forms of later interpretation. But as I feel my way back, it seems rather that I am aware of the rich texture and pattern of a tapestry that was being woven on the loom of my life. I was not passive in the operation, but co-operative, and the design is rich in colour and movement, informing my later reflective and theological thinking.

Of course it is easier to make connections in retrospect, though I must take care not to impose a quite different and alien theological system upon the raw material of childhood experience. But it is difficult for me *not* to see the pattern that took me from my seventh to my sixteenth year. And from that time to the present there is a consistent threefold pattern of spirituality flowing through the personal and communal solitude of my experience.

COSMIC MYSTERY: GOD THE FATHER

There is a powerful, basic reality from which all else flows, and that reality is grounded in the mystery of Being we call God. In the Eastern Orthodox tradition, God the Father is the Fount of deity, and the Son and Spirit are the 'two hands' of the Father. My childhood awareness was alive with this one basic reality, and unity was its hallmark. It was not a monolithic block which was static and unresponsive, but a manifestation of unity which possessed within itself, and released from itself, a cosmic diversity and fecundity. The whole creation was alive with its life – a basic, fundamental unity which overflowed in earth, sea and sky, in animate life and rational creatures – and reverberated in my own childlike soul.

This fundamental childhood awareness was the spring of my religious experience. And it was from the heart of this experience that my later understanding of theology emerged. It was not distinctively Christian in a negative, exclusive or partisan sense, but rather inclusive and universal. It was, I believe, the basic, experiential awareness from which all creative religious thought emerges into language and communication.

I am not implying, of course, that this experience was unchristian or pantheistic. But I think the very sound and feel of what I have said may cause some Christians to feel that there is a pagan resonance about it. If that is the case, I would suggest that our western cast of mind is at fault and not the experience or the theology involved. I think the same people would feel uneasy about much of the Psalter, (e.g. Psalm 104), and with a dynamic theology of the Old Testament.

We have become so familiar with the word *God* that we hardly know what it means. Certainly, the word is meaningless to many people who are by no means lacking in spiritual discernment. They are among the people who are today more spiritually sensitive, and filled with more humanitarian compassion than many professing Christians. And then there are Christians of the charismatic type, both Catholic and Protestant, who use the word in a familiar and 'matey' sense, emptying it of the numinous and awe-ful quality it possesses in scripture. It was no 'pal' with whom Jacob wrestled at the brook Jabbok on that mysterious night of revelation; and the display of divine glory that appeared to Moses in the burning bush and to Isaiah in the temple struck those prophetic characters with reverential awe and holy fear.

This childhood awareness and experience of God the Father was simply 'there' and 'here'. I could use the words *transcendent* and *immanent*, but it does not seem right, in this context, to introduce philosophical language into an experience in which I want to communicate immediacy. He was 'there' in the sense of the *givenness* of the experience. It did not depend on my knowledge, action or participation; it did not come at my bidding or go at my willing. It did not compel attention in the sense of coercion, but certainly did provoke and inspire breathless wonder and adoration. The 'thereness' and 'givenness' of the mystery was much of its glory, for it was before I came into being, and would be after I had departed.

It was 'here' in the sense that there was some kind of personal participation, and responsive dynamic taking place within me. Although I say that it did not compel in the sense of coercion, there was no way in which I could ignore it. I speak of 'it' in the sense of dynamic mystery, but also use the personal pronoun because even as a child I could not conceive of 'it' as being less than 'he'. In my childish thinking the immensity and immediacy of the 'it' was greater than any 'he' (or 'she') I had known. The personal aspect was not something I had thought about directly, but in reflection now, I think I would have related it secondarily to the warmth and love I felt between my parents and myself, and primarily in the experience of the personal which I felt within myself.

In the last sentence I used the words 'warmth' and 'love'. These feelings were not in doubt, for it was mind and heart that were enveloped by, and responded to, this experience. I found and believed that this mystery was gracious and loving. I cannot recall constructing a theodicy, or reconciling 'nature red in tooth and claw' with the rhythmic pounding of the sea, or the glory of the rising and setting sun. But because I lived in the love of my parents, having an emotionally satisfying relationship there, and because I was possessed of a gentle, sensitive spirit which seemed to be native to my nature, I simply acted as if the cosmic mystery was not only all-pervasive, but gracious and loving.

And that brings me to the matter of response. My immediate and basic response to the mystery was the positive acknowledgment of the awareness itself. I mean 'letting it be', allowing the mystery to flow into and up from my very being – a sort of flowing together of the inward and outward manifestations of the one reality. I hesitate to use the word 'prayer', because verbal prayer, and especially petitionary prayer seems not only irrelevant, but improper in the childhood awareness that I am striving to describe. Not that such verbal prayer was impossible but inappropriate. Sighing, singing, or even tears were appropriate, and certainly physical celebration was a real response in terms of running, jumping, dancing or splashing in the sea – but this kind of response was in solitude. The presence of others inhibited such un-selfconscious demonstration. And that is still true.

I cannot recall any moral or ethical sense in terms of law or duty that emerged from this basic experience of cosmic mystery. Love and compassion did not fit into those categories, but were the natural uprising of my response to life's spontaneity, and all this was mixed with joy. The roots of my being were nourished in gentleness and compassion, and I only became aware of duty and obligation as a result of later didactic implication. Moral obligations were 'learned' with social duties and were not part of my immediate awareness of that basic mystery.

EVANGELICAL EXPERIENCE: GOD THE SON

In all I have said above, it is obvious that there is a rich preparation of soil for the seed of the Gospel. I did not come from a Christian home, though it was a loving and stable one. But at ten years of age I began to attend a Baptist Sunday School, and at twelve years of age went, one Sunday evening, to a valedictory service for some young people who had finished their missionary training and were about to set off to their appropriate fields of service. During the service they each bore simple witness to their call and response, and one young woman, who could not have been more than twenty-two years old, spoke with joy accompanied by a radiant face of the way in which she had been apprehended by Christ and challenged to love and serve him. Her enthusiasm lit up in me a longing and response, with a tremendous desire to 'know' this Jesus in a deep and personal way.

Remember, I had always known the pervasive sense of mystery, awe and 'otherness' which so easily related to the understanding of God in the Judaistic tradition which was the background of Jesus' consciousness and teaching. In my longing to know Jesus, I intuitively and consciously linked my childhood experience with the person of Christ, imbibing the teaching of the scripture within the proclamation of the Church.

That evening, following upon the missionary service, I came to a place of decision, surrender and commitment – a conversion, if one can use that term in the experience of a sensitive and trusting twelve-year old boy. Certainly it was an emotional experience, accompanied by tears. But it was also an experience of the mind – a conscious and intelligent espousal of the way of Jesus, and an opening of life and heart to his personal indwelling.

So began a specifically Christian life. From this moment there was a mutual interrelationship between my earlier experience of the mystery of God in the unity and diversity of the cosmic flow, and my evangelical experience. The cosmic mystery could now be almost identified with the God and Father of our Lord Jesus Christ – for the inconsistencies and theological problems inherent in western Protestantism did not immediately arise. And because of the experienced reality in my earlier nature of both mysticism and the evangelical experience of conversion, neither of them could be denied, so there was no head-on collision but a peaceful coexistence until I was exposed to so-called incompatibilities between mystical and prophetic religion.

The great thing about my conversion was that it brought me

into touch with a living evangelical faith which was the centre of New Testament witness, and was the proclamation of the corporate Church. I needed fellowship, sacraments, discipleship and witness. I needed, and found, a place in which I could enter into the love of Christ and follow in his way. This meant learning as a disciple, bearing witness as a redeemed sinner, and showing compassion as one who lived in his love. It meant also entering into the mystical theology of Christ and experiencing union with him in his life, death and resurrection.

I fell in love with Jesus as did St Francis and the early Franciscan fools for Christ, though I did not come to know of them until some time later. The reason why I have been drawn into Franciscan life is because of this very thing, for above all, Francis was a lover of Christ. He was also many other things, but his life and death are inexplicable without the centrality of the living, dying, risen Jesus. And the marks of the stigmata upon his body were but physical manifestations of the wounds of Jesus within his heart — wounds of love, compassion and service to the world.

INDWELLING PRESENCE: GOD THE HOLY SPIRIT

All this was well and good. The Protestant and Reformed tradition in which I found myself enabled me to understand both theologically and experientially the doctrines of the Incarnation and Atonement, and it was with joy that I understood by faith the great question of St Anselm: *Cur Deus Homo?* — Why did God become man? But this same tradition, with its emphasis on the prophetic nature of faith, did not understand

my earlier experiences, nor was it able to expound a pentecostal understanding of the person and work of God the Holy
Spirit, especially in the created order, and in the area of charismatic gifts and graces in the Church.

So at sixteen years of age I found myself searching the pages
of the New Testament with some pertinent questions raised
by pentecostal friends. The result of this was that I earnestly
began to seek a deeper experience of God – not now in the
area of the created order (though the Spirit's indwelling at the
heart of the cosmos was soon to occupy my attention), and not
now in the area of Christology, for some solid work had been
done there, but in the pentecostal experience of the early
Church, in the Acts of the Apostles, and the witness of the
New Testament epistles.

For a lad of sixteen to have such theological concerns may
appear strange in such an irreligious culture as ours, but not
only was there much more spiritual and theological interest
abroad than was admitted by our secular society, but I had been
enveloped by a sense of the spiritual world since my early
childhood. All the early awareness of the presence of God,
combined with an evangelical experience of Christ at twelve
years of age, gave greater impetus to my spiritual pilgrimage,
and I was aware of a missing dimension which was that of the
Holy Spirit.

Then something definite happened which constitutes the third
milestone in my experience, and something was initiated then
which continues as an ongoing quest to this day. The 'something
definite' was an experience of the Holy Spirit which has come
to be known in both Catholic and Protestant circles as 'charismatic'. I was part of a small prayer group which met in the

upper room of a church in Swansea, to wait upon God. One evening, just as the meeting was about to close, I was thrown down from a kneeling posture on to the floor and began to praise and adore God in a language I had never learned. I remember living through the next two hours in a state of joy and inebriation which I have since reckoned was akin to the apostles' experience on the day of Pentecost when they were accused of being full of new wine. It is interesting to note that the Greek text may be translated 'sweet wine' – and sweet it certainly was! I noted in my diary later that this experience lasted for six weeks until I was gently let down into a semblance of normality. The words of Michel Quoist encapsulate the experience well:

> At times, O Lord, you steal over me irresistibly, as the ocean slowly covers the shore,
> Or suddenly you seize me as the lover clasps his beloved in his arms.
> And I am helpless, a prisoner, and I have to stand still.
> Captivated, I hold my breath, the world fades away, you suspend time . . .
> Thank you, Lord, thank you!
> Why me, why did you choose me?
> Joy, joy, tears of joy.

But this was no mere emotional experience, though it did stir my emotional life to its depths. It was an experience which captivated both heart and mind, and at this time my reading became much wider and more catholic. Over the next two or three years I began to read Brother Lawrence, St John of the

Cross, St Augustine – though aware that 'Catholic' writers were frowned upon in the particular part of the Church to which I belonged. There was much less ecumenical understanding than there is now, and the charismatic movement had not got under way at all. At that time, too, I was among the last to be conscripted to military service, and it was quite clear to me that as a Christian I could only be a pacifist. The whole of my religious experience pointed to this. I was pacifist by nature and by conviction.

This situation was not well received at home nor at the church, but though it seemed that my convictions were making me feel *contra mundum* – against the world, yet I had much support, for in the evangelical sections of the Church there is a tremendous warmth and enthusiasm, though, of course, not everyone agreed with my pacifism. This is a conviction which has grown over the years, and though things are not as black and white as they once seemed to be, both theologically or in terms of pacifism, yet I continue to cherish these convictions which were so much part of my young Christian asceticism and discipleship.

The dimension of the Holy Spirit brought me into charismatic freedom, as I came to believe that the charismatic gifts of the early Church had not been withdrawn, but were available today. Also my Catholic reading and experience taught me that I could embrace all that I had learned as a child, so that the mystery of God the Father and the indwelling of the Holy Spirit at the heart of the created order were of a piece with the evangelical experience of forgiveness and compassion in the Lord Jesus.

As I began to recognize the greater catholicity of the Church and the theological integrity of other Christians in Anglican, Roman and (later) Orthodox Churches, I also appreciated increasingly the inspiration of the Holy Spirit in all the aesthetic and academic disciplines, so that music, poetry, art and all creative, literary and scientific endeavour were seen to be manifestations of the same Holy Spirit. This was a revelation to me, and during the course of my reading and sharing I came into contact with the Christian monastic tradition.

A PILGRIM OF FAITH

I have given a Trinitarian shape to my own personal pilgrimage, in terms of childhood mystery, evangelical experience and charismatic awareness, but it is not a shape that is imposed as much as one that has emerged from the concrete realities of my life.

The story continued from those early years into the ministry of the Church of God, as parish priest and university chaplain, and from a memorable 'hermit symposium' (which I'll talk about later) into the Anglican Franciscan tradition of The Society of St Francis.

During my years as an active friar I appreciated my former evangelical upbringing and increasing ecumenical relations within the great catholic communions of the Church. The monastic tradition is much wider than the Franciscan Order, and it was a generous move on the part of The Society of St Francis to allow and encourage me in two six-month experiments with prayer in solitude, first in Dorset in 1982, and then on the edge of the Lleyn Peninsula in 1983-4. It was from there that I returned to become Guardian of Glasshampton monastery in 1984, until my departure to test seriously the hermit life in 1990.

I continue this story in the next chapter, but I would say here that I do not have any ambitions or visions to found or lead a new reform or tradition. My hut life is simple, with prayer, study and manual work as the basic pattern, seeing a few people each month, and continuing to communicate in areas of prayer and spirituality on behalf of others who are on the same pilgrimage. Scripture, the Psalms, Eucharist and silence are my joyful disciplines under the Holy Spirit and I am increasingly grateful to my own Order for our reciprocal relationship in love.

As I look back on this pilgrimage I have become more religious and more worldly! I mean that I have increasingly recognized the presence and love of God at the heart of the human quest and longing, and have come to value my own common humanity as very precious. It is on the basis of common humanity that I look towards my brothers and sisters in the world, of whatever colour, class or creed.

There are times when our poor world which God loves seems very vulnerable and precarious, even on the verge of nuclear or ecological catastrophe. Yet I am enabled to hope in God. It is because of all that Trinitarian faith is to me, within the fellowship of the Church, that I can believe that victory remains with Love.

Part 1

THE PATH OF
EXPERIENCE

the Glasshampton
Crucifix

1

Joys and Difficulties of the Hermit Life

Stability is part of my life-style — putting down roots in solitude and staying put! Therefore, I no longer accept any engagements to preach or conduct missions or retreats, but a few people come to see me every month. Recently a sister came to share with me concerning her new life of a much reduced amount of parish and hospital ministry with a great deal of solitude. She was organizing a symposium on 'Living Alone for God', and asked if I would write a paper for the participants.

I did so, and it sparked off a great deal of interest among people who are struggling to integrate some solitude into extremely busy and demanding lives. This is another illustration of the fact that the busiest and most active people in our contemporary society are those who are most drawn towards the inward meaning of the hermit life.

PERSONAL CONTEXT

There is a beautiful picture of St Antony the anchorite given us by St Athanasius. When his friends broke down the gate of his enclosure, after twenty years of solitude, they found that

Antony's body had not deteriorated by his asceticism, but had rather improved. He had not grown fat through lack of exercise, nor dried up from fasting and fighting with powers of darkness. Physically and in disposition of soul he is described as 'all balanced, as one governed by reason and standing in his natural condition.' Antony's physical health remained robust right up to his death fifty years later, when he was still sound in all his senses and vigorous in his limbs. Even his teeth were all there, though worn down to the gums – at about 105 years of age!

I'm not suggesting that we should strive for such physical achievement – indeed, I want to talk about acceptance of our limitations later, but this incident underlines the 'middle way' which seems to me to be the way of Jesus, who neither presented an austere asceticism nor a hedonistic flouting of discipline, but followed a middle path of simplicity, joy and compassion.

Basically, our pattern is that of Jesus, and I am drawn to a particular understanding of the Jesus way. It comes to me in the form of a 'threefold cord which is not quickly broken'. (Ecclesiastes 4:12). Its three strands are these:

1 The desert fathers and mothers who peopled the deserts of Egypt, Arabia and Persia in the fourth century AD, when the Church was forgetting its pilgrim nature and becoming successful and politically manipulated after the early days of persecution.

2 The Celtic tradition, which is my own heritage. This is represented by such monks as Patrick, David, Columba, Samson and the rest who present a theology and spirituality in which grace and nature run together in immense

spontaneity and discipline.

3 The Franciscan spirituality exemplified in the life and teaching of St Francis and his early followers, which is universal in its appeal in a world mesmerized by money, sex and power.

The white threefold cord that holds my Franciscan habit together speaks to me of my forbears in Christ, and it anchors me to Christ himself, for ultimately there is no other pattern for us but the Saviour, whether we seek to pursue an apostolic or eremitic vocation.

I use the term 'hermit', but ask the reader to interpret it in the light of his or her own experience. In my own case it means that (apart from medical visits and an annual visit to my family) I remain in the enclosure on the grounds of Glasshampton monastery where I have two huts: one for living and one which is my chapel and workshop. I see about four or five people a month for counselling and direction, and a monthly visit from the novices who are living at Glasshampton when we celebrate the Eucharist and share our concerns with each other.

I've declared myself, so that you can see the context from which I live and write, and now to the joys and difficulties which are part of my ongoing experience. Joys first.

A NEW MODE OF LIFE

The first thing that the hermit encounters is a change of tempo. There is a slowing down, a letting go, a finding of a new rhythm, and hopefully, this will mean learning to 'breathe with creation'. Clock time will give way to seasonal time. Light and darkness will come to mean more than monastic bells! This is all gain but it takes some getting used to. I am glad I had two periods of six months' experimentation before I launched out into an open-ended hermit life.

The slowing-down process means that you don't have to live up to external expectations. There are no telephone or door-bell calls, you are not on anyone's agenda, and you have no committee meetings. You don't have to rush from one appoint-ment to another or feel that there is no time to pray, to medi-tate, or even to live at a natural rhythm. There is time for all these – indeed, now you have all the time in the world, for you are totally available to God, and even the rare interviews are in the context of contemplative prayer. You get the feeling that this is how human beings ought to live.

On my last diocesan mission before going off for my second period of six months' solitude, I was leading a discussion group where two young Hindu students asked me what I was going to 'do' during the period. 'Nothing,' I replied, 'absolutely nothing.' They laughed with glee, saying, 'That is exactly the right answer!' They understood, while the Christians in the group needed patient explanation. Of course I 'did' many things, but they could all be set aside to be available to God alone, in the communion of love – that was what 'nothing' meant.

You may not find it easy to let go, but the scariness of it soon gives way to the delight of waking and sleeping, working and watching, eating and fasting – all according to your own internal rhythm, for you will have to learn to listen to your own heartbeat, co-operate with your own breathing, and find your own tempo. It will be a new discovery of the Holy Spirit dwelling within your spirit, and from that depth you will (perhaps for the first time), become aware of God's indwelling, and live according to its pulse.

You will soon realize that the rising and setting of the sun, the waxing and waning of the moon, the ebbing and flowing of the tides, the rise and fall of the sap, the cyclical changing of the seasons — all these will become part of your new rhythm. This rhythm will guide the pattern of your day, and will take the place of the imposed timetable which previously dictated your movements. It is a reversal to a more primitive awareness of rhythm and change which we westerners have largely lost. Therefore, it presents a radical change for the one living alone for God — it means moving at his pace and according to his mode, and has a discipline of its own.

DIVIDING THE DAY

This does not mean a complete abandonment of order, but it does mean that the order and system which you work out for yourself arises now from within, and from the mood and pattern of nature. It is not artificial, mechanistic and dependent on an external work routine. I have a pattern, a system, and a flexible timetable, but it is one which is born of the natural rhythms and changes with the changing seasons, especially the times of dawn and sunset.

The working out of eremitical freedom leads me to make space each day for the threefold division of prayer, study and manual work. My rising and retiring times remain constant through the year, but the shape of the day may change according to season, demands, mood or discernment of inward leading. Let me lay out my present timetable:

4.30 am	Contemplative prayer
6.30 am	Ablutions, breakfast, SSF Morning Prayer
9.00 am	Morning work (garden, bookbinding/prayer stools/ icon mounting)
12.30 pm	Midday Prayer and main meal
2.30 pm	Afternoon work (study, writing, correspondence)
4.30 pm	Cup of tea, reading, SSF Evening Prayer
6.00 pm	Two hours for unspecified tasks (see * below), bread and honey
8.00 pm	Compline and retire

* Evening hours may be used for walking, listening to music or anything missed during the day. The morning and afternoon periods are often interchanged because of occasional visitors or special writing commitments. Working in the vegetable garden, outdoor painting, walking and such activities vary according to season. The wonderful thing is that I can drop my spade, close my book or lay aside my manuscript or correspondence if I feel the Lord calling me into prayerful communion at any time. I am only here for love of Him.

CONTEMPLATIVE DIMENSION

It is clear that the contemplative attitude is primary, towards which the hermit's life must be oriented. This is basically 'experiencing God' at all levels of life, and this includes body, mind and spirit, no less our emotional and intellectual lives. I keep abreast of current spirituality teaching and methods in my study and research, but the actual 'doing' of contemplation the first two hours of my day, consists mainly of using the *Jesus Prayer*, which leads me to imageless silence.

Liturgical offices with the basic psalmody and the Sunday Eucharist all anchored in holy Scripture are also integral to the life of prayer. Experimentation with different methods and techniques of meditation are an important way of deepening our awareness of the fullness of Christ.

Increasingly I find myself growing towards a greater understanding of the cosmic nature of Christ's person and work, and the reflection of his light in all that is best in the world's contemplative teachings.

The fruit of all this is (I trust) a personal growth in humility and maturity which is offered to God in contemplative prayer and intercession, and in counselling, writing and teaching in the sharing of a spirituality of compassion and love.

I find increasing joy in the personal pilgrimage which deepens my own life of prayer in parallel with the sheer 'ordinariness' of daily repetitive living. This personal journey is caught up in the corporate life of my own Franciscan Order, the wider Church and the human concerns of our world. The personal and corporate complement each other, and my hermit vocation is 'our' vocation as it flows from and returns to the world of humankind.

The true goal of contemplation of God is the transformation of the whole cosmos through the redeeming work of Christ, and I feel that I play a small but vital part in that great universal movement of love by which God draws all creation into union with Himself. The 'ecstatic' and the 'ordinary' are two sides of the coin of love, and both are represented in my present pilgrimage.

DISCIPLINE

Though I wax eloquent about freedom and spontaneity, these qualities cannot exist without discipline. This must be self-imposed and voluntary, though in my case it is worked out with my spiritual director. I have 'three wise men' as counsellors. Fr Donald Allchin is my spiritual director, Brother Anselm is my 'buffer brother' within the SSF Chapter, and Brother Damian is my provincial minister. So whatever I work out with Fr Donald is shared with the other two, and the Chapter is kept abreast of developments (and asked for permissions!).

Because I did two six-month trial runs and am now into the fifth year of solitude, there are no radical departures from what we laid down at the beginning, save that the first year meant that I laid aside (as well as all engagements) my writing, and saw no one for counselling. During the second year I began to write again, and then to see a few people a month. This has continued and the balance now seems right.

I would interpret the word *discipline* in the light of my *discipleship* in Christ, seeing it as something by which I grow in awareness and love of God, my fellows and myself.

So much for joys – what about the difficulties? Well here goes:

SOLITUDE

Solitude is a positive joy, but I must admit that there is an element of loneliness in it. I miss people, for although I am fundamentally solitary, I am also gregarious, a communicator and a preacher. It is a salutary thing to realize that the world and the Church are getting on very well without me. I am not needed, not indispensable, and Glasshampton's ministry continued in all its parts when I had laid aside the Guardianship.

I love sharing my joys, am helped in sharing my sorrows, and find great encouragement and self-affirmation in helping others. 'I need to be needed!' At first there was an end to all that, and as I've said elsewhere, I'm a fan of Barbra Streisand, and especially of her version of 'People who need people are the luckiest people in the world.'

There is a certain deprivation in being single, celibate and living alone, and simple honesty demands its recognition. Acknowledging it and coming to terms with it are part of my human and Christian quest, and though I have used the term deprivation, I must also admit that in the context of the experience of God's dynamic love and personal call, the element of deprivation is lost in fulfilment and joy.

DISCERNMENT, DARKNESS AND HUMOUR

Then there are difficulties in matters of discernment. What is the will of God? How does one differentiate between the dark night of the soul and simple depression? How does one know when to be firm and when to be flexible in life-style, relationships, and the shape of one's hermit life?

I've linked discernment and humour, for it seems to me that the above questions must be faced with a certain humour about oneself, not taking oneself too seriously, with the ability to laugh at the ridiculous vocation to the hermit's life.

If I can chuckle at my problems and be simply human and commonsensical about them, then this is the close second requirement to holiness in the spiritual journey.

Yet, although Martin Luther said that one should laugh at and mock the devil, real spiritual darkness must be taken seriously. The gift of discernment of spirits is one of the charisms (divinely inspired powers) of the Holy Spirit, and it is especially relevant to the hermit life, for in the desert tradition the hermit is the special target of demonic powers.

This does not simply mean that the hermit is open to spiritual trauma and attacks of dark psychic forces, but that there is an objective power of evil which is personal and to which St Paul calls our particular attention, that we might be clothed in the whole armour of God. 'For our struggle is not against enemies of blood and flesh, but against the rulers, against the authorities, against the cosmic powers of this present darkness, against the spiritual forces of evil in the heavenly places.' (Ephesians 6:12).

Scripture must be the bedrock of the hermit life, of course, but I have often found it of great help to read it with St John of the Cross or Carl Jung's teaching on *Individuation*. This helps me to know and understand myself in relation to God and others, and sorts out the shape of the 'dark night' and pattern of my own psyche.

Certainly I keep in touch with my director, but a hermit

needs psychic maturity and firm common sense mixed with humour in order to continue the journey.

MORTALITY

I've always acknowledged the need to recognize and confront my mortality. It is not wise to underestimate its importance. Into the third year of my solitude I had an 'episode' of severe vertigo, blood pressure, and other symptoms from which I've not yet totally recovered, and it has taught me a great deal which could have come no other way.

Sickness of body, psychic fragility and the 'little deaths' along the way all contribute to a realistic view of who and what we are as human creatures. St Francis trod this path deep into the dark valley.

I must admit that I find difficulty in not being physically healthy, I am impatient at lack of concentration and resistant to submitting to another of those 'little deaths' that bring me closer to those inevitable words: 'Into your hands, O Lord, I commend my spirit.' But this is the way of it, and together with the difficulties comes the joy of being loved and sustained in the darkness by the Lord who has travelled the whole way before me.

I've preached and written often that the way of Christian discipleship follows the pattern of Jesus' death and resurrection. Now the experience is impinging more and more upon me at every level of my being, and I must walk that way in simple trust, the Lord being my helper. And I must embrace it, not simply be resigned to it, for in such an attitude lies further maturity and growth in love and grace.

It is good that there is grace for every trial, and in the middle of new difficulties new strength is experienced and new joys encountered. One of the things which constantly surprises me (and shouldn't) is that my strength is made perfect in weakness, and others do benefit from a wounded healer precisely because of his or her vulnerabilities.

THE HERMIT AND THE COMMUNITY

The hermit's relationship with community continues to play an important part in the lives of both. There is the official understanding between the brother or sister with the wider Order which needs always to be clear and affirmative, and there are the personal relationships between the hermit and other brothers and sisters.

If the vocation can be seen in a wider dimension than 'doing my own thing' then it will be productive. Indeed it is difficult to see how the hermit vocation can flourish unless there is encouragement and affirmation from the chapter and community. But difficulties seem inevitably part of the way for many people in the hermit tradition. This makes me a bit scared that my relationship with my own community continues to be so warm and good. The experience of the reader may be different, and I must not speak too soon!

The situation of the hermit who is not a 'religious' is different, but even then there is the bishop to whom vows are made, and the circle of praying/helping friends which is indispensable. So if these relationships are good then the hermit does not have to ask, 'Is this a vocation or a dead end?' Of course there will be the perplexities and criticisms of people not acquainted with the desert tradition both inside and outside the Church. That has to be accepted, and if it appears that the hermit life, in their opinion, is non-productive and not fulfilling a 'relevant function' in our frenetic society, well, the hermit must be content to let that be. You can't please everyone! In any case there is an increasing number of people who look with yearning to a life-style that is simple, poor and honest, and who draw on the hermit's life of contemplation as a pattern for their own existence. But we must be on our guard lest our vocation becomes invalid because of our own loss of vision, or because a hidden deterioration takes place which is concealed until it can be hidden no longer.

That is why the channels of communication must be kept open — first of all between the hermit and the Lord in simplicity, integrity and love, then between the hermit and the community, which includes the spiritual director, fellow-believers and friends.

I have only touched on some joys and difficulties of living alone for God in the hermit life. I conclude this on a day in which I have spent two hours planting a seed bed, an hour listening to *Bach's St Matthew Passion* in the context of the Eucharist and spring loveliness on this Feast of the Annunciation to the Virgin Mary. Therefore I conclude with her beautiful words:

Here am I, the servant of the Lord;
Let it be with me according to your word.
(Luke 1:36)

The Prayer Hut

2

Describing the Place

PREPARING THE WAY

The people of God were desert dwellers. They had no abiding place on earth, and in their early days lived a nomadic life in tents (Genesis 18:1). This sense of continuing pilgrimage underlined their wilderness sojournings, for even God himself tabernacled among them and moved on with them (Exodus 25:8f). In the prophetic tradition the school of the prophets under Elisha built their huts of wood (2 Kings 6:1–4). The desert fathers of the fourth century or earlier lived in caves, wattle huts, and stone and wooden dwellings in Palestine, Syria and Egypt, and so did the Celtic monks and hermits of Britain.

The Orthodox tradition has been more faithful than the Latin Church to the hermit and desert life, and it was clear, when I attended the hermit symposium which was convened at St David's, Wales, in 1975, that the revival of the hermit life in the Western Church drew profound inspiration from the unbroken tradition of the East.

It was at St David's, during that week, that the main thrust of my hermit vocation began in earnest. I was drawn there by an inward yearning and was struck by the simplicity, integrity and reality of the hermit life before my eyes. As I write these words in my hermitage twenty years later, my heart still leaps at the words of Peter Anson which were quoted at that symposium:

> There are always likely to be some men and women who feel that 'material' solitude is essential for their spiritual life. They can no more do without it than without food or drink, and if they are deprived of this isolation their lives become spoilt, cramped and distorted, and they never find their true vocations. The 'born solitary' is drawn to an eremitical life for various reasons, partly natural, partly supernatural . . . They discover that they need to separate themselves from their fellow-creatures in order that their latent powers may have room for expansion and growth, that they may be more fitted to serve mankind generally.*

Between that symposium and actually taking off seriously to test the hermit vocation in 1990, I moved from being a parish priest and university chaplain, entered The Society of St Francis, got busily involved in the ministry and evangelism work of SSF, was allowed to do two six-month periods of solitude, and spent six years as Guardian of Glasshampton monastery.

All the time, in the midst of an enjoyable and busy life in community and ministry, my heart yearned over the solitude spoken of above. So in 1990, I took off with a small caravan,

* A. M. Allchin (ed.), *Solitude and Communion, Papers on the Hermit Life*, given at St David's, Wales, by Orthodox, Roman and Anglican contributors, (Oxford: Fairacres Publication, 1977), p. 70.

and set it down in the plum orchard on the grounds of Tymawr convent. For three very wonderful years I tested the joys and difficulties of the hermit life, surrounded by the beauty of the convent land and the prayers and support of the sisters of The Society of the Sacred Cross.

I must admit, though, that the limitations of a 12' x 6' caravan did constrict me. You can read about some of the humour and trials encountered in my book *Forty Days and Forty Nights*. (Marshall Pickering, 1993)

I was told in 1992 by my GP that I was not to spend another winter without heat, so my plan was to convert a small barn into a cell with a wood-burning stove. But every time I went into the barn to pray towards it I kept hearing the words of Psalm 127:1: 'Unless the Lord builds the house, those who build it labour in vain.'

So in May 1993, after sharing my perplexity with a brother, and agreeing to do nothing until the matter became clear, I was walking across the field next to the barn, and in one moment I was struck with the words: 'You're going back to Glasshampton, aren't you?' 'Yes!' I replied, without hesitation. It was as simple, as immediate and as clear as that. I wish all guidance was as simple.

HERMITAGE AT GLASSHAMPTON

So in September 1993 I gave away the caravan, returned to Glasshampton, and down below the vegetable garden where there was already a hut 10' x 8' (which is now my chapel and working hut), we set up a new living hut 12' x 8', and a loo-cum-toolshed hut measuring 4' x 4', and here I am. It is not as spartan and austere as it was as I have a source of light and winter heat, and I have more space, but the simplicity remains, and that is appreciated by myself and by the small stream of visitors who come to see me each month.

The enclosure measures approx. 75 x 50 feet, is surrounded by trees and shrubs, and faces fields which run down to a wooded area, with the red tower of St Peter's, Astley, rising up in the distance. One brother, Michael, made an *iconostasis* (icon stand) to house the large icon of Our Lady of Vladimir, and it has its place under the trees opposite my living hut. Then Robert fashioned an oak Celtic cross which stands at the door of the chapel hut.

It is an ideal situation, for no one stumbles upon me by accident, yet my door is open for those who need to come. In this way I am freed from the temptation of becoming involved again in over-active ministry.

I feel that this life genuinely participates in the great tradition of the hermit life in the Church, though I continue to learn more of my limitations and failures as I move forward in joy. The surrendering of my active teaching and preaching ministry has its recompense in the way in which my books are received by readers in all denominations, and I increasingly feel that this hidden life of mine is accessible enough for prayer and ministry to others to mingle in the mercy of God.

I owe a great deal to my community SSF, and to the late Mother Mary Clare SLG and Fr Donald Allchin who have given me loving direction over the last nearly two decades. They were both at that memorable hermit symposium, and Mother Mary Clare concluded her paper with words which have become real in my experience and in the Church of our day:

> *The hermit is simply a pioneer . . . in the way of the desert which the whole of humanity must follow of necessity one day, each one according to his measure and his desire. This eremitical vocation, at least embryonically, is to be found in every Christian vocation, but in some it must be allowed to come into its full flowering in the wind of the Spirit. It is not enough to affirm that the thing is good in itself, it is necessary that the Church and society do something so that this life may be realizable, so that each may at least touch it, be it only with the tip of his little finger.**

THE BLESSING OF THE HERMITAGE

After the preparation, erection and fitting-out of the huts were complete, on the Feast of St Francis (4th October) 1993, the brothers accompanied me down from the monastery to the enclosure in procession, and a simple blessing took place as follows:

Blessing of Hermitage

PROCESSION: Following Evensong, the brothers accompany Ramon down to the hermitage enclosure with incense and holy water.

AT HERMITAGE ENTRANCE: In the Name of the Father, and of

---

* *Solitude and Communion*, (op.cit.) p. 76.

the Son, and of the Holy Spirit. *Amen*.

Psalm 121 is said antiphonally.

ENCLOSURE PRAYER: Almighty God, by the power of your Holy Spirit who indwells all creation, and by the grace of our Lord Jesus Christ who has shed his blood for our redemption, cast out all evil powers and influences from this place, that it may manifest the mystery and glory of your divine love. *Amen*.

JERICHO PROCESSION: Brothers process around the inside of the perimeter of the enclosure censing the whole area, arriving back to face the huts.

FACING HUTS: Heavenly Father, bless this hermitage, and your servant Ramon, that the life of prayer and love may glorify your name in the world, to the reconciliation of the whole cosmos.

HERMITAGE AND MONASTERY: Unite the prayers of hermitage and monastery in this place, O Lord, that all who live here and all who share our life may enter more deeply into the embrace of your divine compassion, that your name may be praised and adored, Father, Son and Holy Spirit. *Amen*.

Psalm 122 is said antiphonally.

ALL: The grace of our Lord Jesus Christ, and the love of God, and the communion of the Holy Spirit be with us all evermore. *Amen*.

KISS OF PEACE: Brothers exchange the peace with Ramon, and depart.

3

Imagine Yourself . . .

JOURNEY INTO SOLITUDE

There are such things as idle day-dreams, the imaginative painting of scenarios of possibility which are not only time-wasting and counter-productive, but which can be dangerous if you allow yourself to enter into dark imaginations of power, lust or fortune. But there is a healthy use of the imagination which has an inspirational source and allows the dreamer to enter into dimensions and potentialities in which his or her creative powers come into play and suggest ways forward to a fulfilment of hidden possibilities and an acceptance of the challenge of the will of God.

It doesn't need to be kept within the bounds of what you think are your humble limitations. For instance, the creative reading of a powerful life-story can inspire you to hopes, longings and challenges which expand your individual horizon and enable you to do in your way what the author did in his or her life. Even off the top of my head I can think of autobiographies and biographies which have inspired, motivated, called and scared me out of my wits! If your reading is creative, it is not simply a matter of perusing such books for recreation, duty or sheer enjoyment (and there's nothing wrong there), but of getting inside the books, inside the skin of the writers, and living in, through and with them the adventures, escapades, spills and thrills of their physical, mental and spiritual journeys.

So let me lay before you a simple scenario which is so ridiculous, so way out, so impossible for some contemporary people, that they would laugh it out of court. And yet this same experimental invitation would cause other people to hold their breath in wonder, in amazement, in profound yearning, so that they would give almost everything to be able to accept the invitation which would challenge and revolutionize their life.

The trouble is that the person who most needs it, who would most profit by it, and who yearns most profoundly for it, is often the very person who is not able to take up the offer because of relationships, family, career, job-structure or 101 other obstacles.

Well, this is where vision and imagination come in. The very possibility of an imaginative journey with me in this book, and especially in this chapter, may well clear away the stones and rubble blocking up the springs of your deepest self, so that you may become aware of the voices of ancient glory and pain which are deeper than your individuality, and echo the mystery of God.

Making such an imaginative journey may well lead you to experience the indwelling of the Holy Spirit and to find yourself borne along by the powerful will of God which has always yearned for you and called you, although you have allowed your deepest yearnings to be desensitized and your spiritual hearing to be dulled by the materialism of our present world system.

A SIMPLE EXPERIMENT

I wonder if I have built up your expectations to such a degree that you will be either astonished or disappointed at what I envisage as a fulfilment of the above promise — for the most wonderful thing is so simple.

It is so simple an experiment, so basic and poor that it becomes frightening, ridiculous and impossible to some minds. That is why the words 'many are called but few are chosen' (Matthew 22:14) suits this invitation very well. The man or woman who would scorn or cast aside the opportunity that I am about to describe makes a comment on the validity of their own lives as well as their understanding of human life itself. It is about time I issued the invitation.

Suppose you came across the following advertisement in your Christian paper:

> Brother Ramon SSF proposes to set up a six-month experiment on living in solitude, involving the basic elements of prayer, study and manual work. Life and diet would be simple, accommodation in a single, solitary hut during the week, with Sunday sharing in Eucharist, instruction, guidance and fellowship. The season would be during spring and summer and three men and three women would be accepted. If you think that God may be calling you to undertake such a period, write for details.

Many readers wouldn't give it a second thought; many would read it with positive interest and realize it would not be for them; many would look at it longingly and (rightly or wrongly) turn it down because of time, responsibilities, fears or inadequacies. But some would scramble to know more – and most of these would be refused a place.

THE BASIC FRAMEWORK

Let me describe the experiment I have in mind, and then ask where you would find yourself among those refusing or accepting such a venture.

The idea would be to have seven hut hermitages (or small caravans) out of sight and earshot of each other, with a central chapel hut. Each brother and sister (called Companions) would be responsible for their own domestic and working needs during the week, and would live in solitude from Monday to Saturday, according to a determined timetable which would be firm enough for discipline and flexible enough for spontaneity. Saturday evening and Sunday would contain the communal or sharing aspects of the life something after the following pattern:

Saturday

5.00 pm   Evening prayer and Service of Light
6.00 pm   Communal instruction from the desert tradition or an aspect of contemporary spirituality with discussion
8.00 pm   Meal with music
9.00 pm   Compline, meditation and return to huts

Sunday

7.00 am   Holy Eucharist

40

8.00 am   Talking breakfast
9.00 am   Three one-hour pastoral interviews with
          Companions, involving problems, joys, study
          discussion, reading guidance, planning of manual
          work and personal prayer
12.30 pm Midday prayer and talking lunch
2.00 pm   Interviews with remaining three Companions
5.30 pm   Evening prayer and The Jesus Prayer
7.00 pm   Supper with music
8.00 pm   Compline, meditation and return to huts

The Companions, apart from their one-hour interviews, will have time for sharing or walking together during the Sunday which they may appreciate after the whole week of silence, though it is best to be extempore about this as some people are drawn deeper into silence as the weeks pass, while others begin in profound silence and move into some sharing on Sundays.

You will note (in chapter one) the kind of manual work that I undertake, but you may begin to develop a new skill during the months which will give you great joy. As to study, there would be a basic reading plan which all Companions would undertake, but there would be specific areas that you could cover as long as the study is relevant to the journey. Since there are no academic examinations in view, you could take to heart the words of St Theresa of the Child Jesus:

If I had been a priest I should have made a thorough study of Hebrew and Greek so as to understand the thought of God as he has vouchsafed to express it in our human language.

The weekday timetable may be based on that which I use, though it can be flexible and tailor-made after consultation. The six Companions may respond and react to solitude in six different ways, and certainly not according to expectations! It is not possible to forecast as solitude casts a person into a radical reorientation, exposing him or her to heights and depths hitherto unimagined.

This is why my pastoral door would be open any morning, though not for social calls! Under God, silence is the best teacher, and the daily mix of prayer, scripture, study and manual work would provide a framework of a simple life in which the daily recitation of the Psalter would reflect all the moods of the Companion. The wise advice of the desert father was: 'Go and sit in your cell — your cell will teach you all things.'

WHO WOULD RESPOND?

Now what kind of person would be likely to respond to my invitation and challenge — I mean not simply to *imagine* oneself on such a voyage of self-discovery, but actually to venture on the journey? I will not here deal with those who would scorn or be indifferent to such an experiment because you would not be reading a book like this if you were among them. But what about the following?

1 *'I don't have the spiritual resilience or courage to face it.'* Jesus gave warnings about those who set out on a discipleship path and were not able to complete it or did not count the

cost beforehand (Luke 14:25–33). It is as well to realize
your own limitations and be honest about your fears, but if
this is a concrete or imaginative journey God wants you to
make in faith, he will sustain and energize your venture. It
is not about self-reliance and asceticism, but about the
mercy and grace of God's enabling.

2 *'It's physically too demanding.'* You've got the idea! I'm not
inviting you to a luxurious retreat house with prepared food
and showers laid on. The hut (or caravan) would be basic
and simple (though with a source of heat) and you would be
responsible for your own food and cleanliness. I remember
my first exposure to solitude in my twenties – two weeks
in a lonely cottage in Ilfracombe, and two weeks in a
caravan in the country. The joy of spartan simplicity and
complete freedom initiated me into a deeper life of human
awareness of the divine Love – a real trial run!

3 *'I couldn't face such solitude.'* Are you afraid? Is such an
exposure a threat to your very being? Again, it is good to
know this about yourself – but have you tried it? You affirm
the warm human need for friends, for human love, for
ongoing and fulfilling relationships. But sooner or later you
will have to face yourself. It can be very frightening and
that is why you must not enter into a protracted period of
solitude without help. You will have a lifeline and the
possibility of returning at any point, though there must be
the *intention* of seeing it through. My first six months of
solitude began with such an intention whatever happened,
and this was itself a source of strength – though it was the
second six-month period that was the fierce one!

4 *'I don't have the time/space/money for such a pilgrimage.'* Well,

that is why I am proposing an 'imaginative journey' lived out in snatches of days or weeks when possible. You know your own time; you know how much your family/work needs you; you know your own financial situation. But if you could get leave of family and work, and if you could afford not to earn for the period (the actual cost would be less than your usual life-style), then such a 'sabbatical' could revolutionize your life.

5 *'I want this more than anything else.'* This is a difficult one, for there is a certain kind of person who ought not to undertake such a journey, mainly because he or she is psychically unsuited. There certainly would be some of these who would respond to such an advertisement, and would be refused. I am indicating the danger of solitude, of the wrong kind of cutting yourself off from your fellows because you don't get on with them, because you want to run from the real world into a pseudo-spirituality, or because you want to return to the security of the womb. Solitude is not an advisable option for you. But if your 'wanting' is wholesome, and sounds from your creative depths, perhaps as a new phenomenon at this time of your life, it may place you within the last category.

6 *'Such an invitation reverberates within me at a level I cannot understand.'* At last, here is something in the nature of a call, a vocation, a demand which has to be responded to. Some people have, from childhood, felt a vocation to inwardness and solitude; some have included periods of solitude throughout their lives; some have crushed their early love of solitude in frenzied activity but are now hearing the call again; some, after years of busyness, wandering, searching

and bewilderment, are at last being moved in the direction of solitude; and some are in the last decade of their lives and want to experience the dimension of eternity.

IMAGINE YOURSELF . . .

At the beginning of this chapter you were asked to make a journey in imagination, and this chapter may have helped you to see the immense value in doing so. Continue this imaginative journey, then, using token day or weekend periods to this end. You will find that this practice will open up new channels of creative prayer and sharing that will benefit your interior life of contemplation and your exterior life of discipleship and fellowship.

Such imaginative thinking may also put your feet on the road to a substantial period of solitude, perhaps not necessarily in the shape suggested in this chapter, but in a way which would suit you. Why not discuss it with your spiritual director or soul friend? The remaining chapters of this book will feed such imaginative thinking, and will indicate the heights and depths of real experience in God and solitude. If you become a companion on this way, you will understand anew the words of Robert Frost:

Two roads diverged in a wood,
I took the one less travelled
And that has made all the difference.

Part II

THE PRACTICE
OF SPIRITUALITY

Under the Enclosure Cherry Tree

4

Making a Retreat

THE MOTIVE OF RETREAT

A few years ago, conducting a Franciscan evangelistic mission in Bracknell, I was asked to give a talk to staff at the Weather Forecasting Centre. I had a great welcome, and it was a good time – somewhat hilarious as many fringe mission encounters turn out to be. But this one contained a lively confrontation. It took place during the question time and went approximately like this:

Fellow: My colleague downstairs says that you people run away from life.

Me: Does he? Well, go and fetch him.

F: Oh, . . . he's not there now; it's his lunch time.

Me: Are you sure it's your colleague? It wouldn't be you thinking that, by any chance?

F: No, no. It was my colleague.

Me: Well I'll tell you what we'll do. I'm here for a fortnight. You tell him that I'd like to have a dialogue with him here one lunch time. We'll give an open invitation and he can say anything and make out any case he likes, and I'll answer him. And we'll see who is running away. Will you do that? And if he doesn't respond, perhaps I'll come and find him. Will you do that?

F: Yes, I'll tell him.

Some chuckling went on, and we amicably brought the meeting to a close. But I heard no more from the Weather Centre, and I did not carry out my threat.

There's no smoke without fire, and I'm sure it could be said that among the many abuses and corruptions of the monastic life some men and women have retreated into the cloister because of fear. They could not face the world, could not survive among their peers, so ran into the bosom of mother Church! And what a hash they made of it there, destroying their own lives and negatively affecting the corporate life around them.

The word *retreat* seems to indicate that behaviour, doesn't it? The idea of withdrawal as running away, defeatism, fear of conflict or confrontation. The word itself is neutral, and depending on the motivation, it may have those negative meanings. An army may retreat in disarray, in fear and total collapse. Or it may retreat to recuperate, to reconsider, to regroup – in order to attack more effectively.

Of course, negative factors may be such that a person or group need to 'down tools' and retreat from the public eye to ask basic questions about low morale, failure, corruption or ineffectiveness. The Church at times is brought to its knees in helplessness, spiritual bankruptcy and loss of vision, so that a time of retreat is called for leading to repentance and renewal of life and vitality.

The upside of retreat may be wholly positive. Retreat is to enter into the secret place, the trysting place with the beloved, the meeting with a friend, the disciple's learning or training place with the master, a soldier's place of withdrawal after a long and weary battle, or a servant's return after an exhausting task, for recuperation and renewal.

THE CALL OF GOD

The call into the desert, the wilderness, the cave of the heart, sounds throughout the prophetic story of the Old Testament, beginning with Abraham, through the fantastic stories of Jacob, Joseph, Moses, Elijah and up to the wilderness asceticism of John the Baptist. God lays hold upon patriarch or prophet, stirs up a strange restlessness, engineers a mystical confrontation, imparts a prophetic call and drives him out from the desert retreat into the camp of the enemy or into confrontation with the wicked king. But first of all there must take place an exposure of the prophetic soul with the searing holiness of God.

This call to retreat, confrontation, vision and return is rooted in the Old Testament, and comes to flower and fruit in the New. Mary's call is a profoundly interior one, and her place of retreat is the cave of the heart, and the mystery of the womb. Saul of Tarsus stubbornly resisted the call until he was powerfully and effectively confronted on the Damascus road, blinded, converted and transformed into Paul the apostle. Immediately after his conversion he obeyed the interior call and retreated into the desert of Arabia where the mystical vision of the indwelling Christ was burned into his soul. And St John the Divine, during the bloody persecution of the Church under Nero and Domitian, around AD 94, was exiled in enforced retreat on a barren, rocky little island off the coast of Asia Minor called Patmos.

In all these cases it was God who stirred up the human heart, drew the believer into the geographical and existential wilderness, in order to purify and illumine the soul and impart a revelation and vision in order that the burden of prophecy or apostolic vision of holiness should be carried back to the marketplace.

Jesus himself was the supreme fulfilment of Old Testament prophetic and messianic expectation, and he treasured a hidden, interior contemplative life, dwelling continually in the Holy Spirit and in the love of the Father. Yet he also sought the geographical solitude of the wilderness, the desert places, the high mountain, often spending the whole night in prayer, offering up loud cries and tears of adoration, intercession and inexpressible groanings.

THE PATTERN OF JESUS

This call of God, woven into the pattern of Jesus is the basis of our life of prayer, and in Mark 6:30ff we find the call into the desert as the prerequisite for the Church's mission:

> The apostles gathered around Jesus, and told him all that they had done and taught. He said to them, 'Come away to a deserted place all by yourselves and rest awhile.' For many were coming and going, and they had no leisure even to eat. And they went away in the boat to a deserted place by themselves.

If we trace the pattern of Jesus it will become clear why we must respond to this call to desert retreat, and the purpose for which the call continues to sound. There are at least four reasons:

1 *Jesus went into retreat for rest and renewal*. This is the simplest reason, because his ministry was exhausting, with the constant demands of the world's pain drawing on his spiritual and physical resources. When Elijah dropped exhausted at

Horeb, the Angel of the Lord sustained him with food and caused him to sleep. We need all that, and we also need a psychological retreat from our materialistic and frenetically active marketplace society. We need a place and time to unwind, to become passive, open, gentle, receptive, and only then can our spirits be refreshed, renewed and revitalized.

2 *Jesus went into retreat for guidance and direction.* Before he chose his twelve disciples, he spent all the previous night on the mountain in prayer. People come to Glasshampton on retreat before a new venture, in preparation for marriage, after a broken relationship, or to listen for a new life-direction. We don't have to demand, harass and cajole God to reveal his will. When the right time comes he will make it clear *if* we are in a receptive place with an open heart. 'Be less demanding and be more receptive' is the message of retreat.

3 *Jesus went into retreat to confront the powers of darkness.* The Gospels tell us that he was 'led' and that he was 'driven'. This seems to contradict the first reason, but for everything there is a season, and if we follow him, the time will come for our confrontation, for our conflict with the darkness within and outside us. Only in this way could Jesus take the measure of his own soul, wrestling with the powers of darkness against the temptations to find some other way to redeem the world. He was tempted by Satan to take the way of the material economist, the politician or the wonder worker. Both in the wilderness and at Calvary, Jesus confronted the devil face to face. He engaged fully in spiritual warfare, put all the powers of darkness to flight by his death and resurrection, making of them an open spectacle and bringing them into captivity and submission (Hebrews

2:14; 1 John 3:8; Colossians 2:15). There is no doubt to the man or woman who enters into prayer and solitude that there are not only interior dark psychic powers to reckon with and overcome, but that there is objective, cosmic darkness which presses upon the believer and the Church, and stands behind the menacing international conflicts of our world, pouring in evil, malice, subterfuge and cruelty. Christ once for all, in his life and death, confronted and overcame these dark powers for us, and now he desires to accomplish the same work in us. Our response to his call to solitude and retreat is to enter this dimension of conflict and victory. Those who respond to the call will be empowered by the Holy Spirit in such conflict (Ephesians 6:10–12), and in that way we shall share Christ's sufferings more profoundly, uniting our love with his redemptive work for the salvation of the world. (Philippians 3:10).

4 *Jesus went into retreat to contemplate the glory of God.* This is the primary and basic reason to obey the call to prayer. It is not simply to rest, regaining strength and vision, not only to seek guidance for the direction of your life, not even just to enter more deeply into the redemptive work of Christ in facing the powers of darkness which threaten our world. All these reasons are valid and important. But the divine call is to contemplate the glory, the beauty, the wonder of the mystery of God's love. According to St John of the Cross, the difference between meditation and contemplation, is that in meditation we play our part in giving our mind and imagination to the images, parables, stories, wisdom and teaching that is part of our revealed Faith, and God helps and illumines our efforts in prayer, study and communication.

But in contemplation we let go all the discursive methods of the mind, we stop the cerebral *work* of thinking our way to God, we are unable to go on with all our busy prayers and piety – we simply become still. That is what St Seraphim meant when he said:

I tell you, when God visits us in his ineffable goodness we must be still, even from prayer. In prayer the soul utters words of speech, but when the Holy Spirit has come, you must be in complete silence.

This has to do with the deeper reaches of prayer, and there is no clear line of demarcation between meditation and con-templation. We are weaned slowly over many years, with a mixture of meditative and contemplative prayer, but when the mind truly descends to the heart in prayer, we are given glimpses of unitive glory, caught up into the wonder of adoration, laid low by the smiting of the Holy Spirit, until we are down and on our faces before the unutterable glory of God.

It is no easy path and for the beginner there are many 'sensible' joys and delights of grace in prayer to lead us deeper, and then we are confronted with a twofold dark night which lies between us and the ever-deepening life of contemplation and ultimate union. I shall deal with this in chapter twenty, but I mention it here for it is an integral part of the wider purpose of retreat. The withdrawal into the mystery of the dazzling darkness of God is a long way ahead, but the beginnings of this path is when you respond to the call of God to make a simple retreat filled with his presence in love and prayer.

PRACTICAL ASPECTS OF RETREAT

Retreats are not for élite groups of esoteric people, but cater for all kinds of Christians. They teach a spirituality that spills over into evangelism, healing, social work, peace and justice as well as offering the basic framework of meditative practice and silence.

A retreat may take place within a day held at your local church, or it could stretch to a three months' Ignatian retreat, or even the kind of exposure to solitude which I've outlined in chapter three – 'Imagine Yourself. . .' But we usually think of a retreat lasting a weekend from Friday evening to Sunday, or the inside of a week from Sunday to Saturday. If you are making a first retreat, it would be wise for you to choose a guided retreat where there is a framework of addresses and a sharing of worship, and if this can be organized from your own church or prayer group, or with a friend, all the better.

You may find yourself attracted to the kind of creative retreat which offers meditation through music, poetry-making, healing, painting, calligraphy or journalling. There are demanding retreats of a fasting week (participants are vetted and warned – one of our friars was stopped on the third day!), or even a gentle introduction to NT Greek or OT Hebrew – but these latter are for high-fliers! The individually-guided retreat is increasingly popular, with much silence, working with Scripture, and twice-daily interviews with the director (not my choice).

All these retreats are often over-subscribed. A 'Merton' retreat which I conducted at Cropthorne, Pershore, had to be done twice. After my share of attending and conducting retreats I found it best to make a solitary retreat, either in a monastic house sharing the daily Eucharist, or completely on my own in a private place. You can see the rich possibilities if you have a share in a retreat such as that described in chapter six.

First retreatants have to face the problem of silence until they realize that it is not a problem but a joy, and that only comes by experience. It is extraordinary how people get to know one another better in companionable silence than in busy, talking conferences, especially at meals. There is usually a talking area anyway, and smiling is not restricted, nor the occasional necessary word.

What you should take, the customs of the retreat house, the kind of programme, the cost, and other necessary information, is available on request, and there are often reductions for 'broke' or unemployed people, and sometimes self-catering facilities.

Because of the ecumenical stance of most retreats, it is refreshing to be exposed to new ways of worship, teaching and meditative techniques and liturgy. I made my first confession in the Reformed community in Taizé, shared in the incense-laden atmosphere at Orthodox Vespers at the cathedral at St David's while the 'bones of David' were being venerated, and prayed in tongues at an Orthodox-Presbyterian liturgy in Edinburgh. A Roman Catholic would find the meaning of retreat expressed beautifully in the words of the Anglican Charles Wesley from the Methodist Hymn Book:

> Silent am I now and still,
> Dare not in Thy presence move;
> To my waiting soul reveal
> The secret of Thy love.

So why don't you join in the joy and the silence and make a retreat?

5

A Worship Corner in Your Home

A PLACE SET APART

In the tenth century, Prince Vladimir of Kiev sent emissaries on a journey to discover the faith he should adopt for his people. After many and varied experiences they arrived in Constantinople where they experienced the celebration of the liturgy in the great Church of Hagia Sophia:

> We knew not whether we were in heaven or on earth, for surely there is no such splendour or beauty anywhere upon earth. We cannot describe it to you: only this we know, that God dwells there among men, and that their service surpasses the worship of all other places. For we cannot forget that beauty.*

It was that experience which caused Prince Vladimir and his people to adopt Byzantine Orthodoxy into Russia in the year 988. And that beautiful quotation sent me to examine the illustration and schematic plan of the immense Church of Hagia Sophia in my *History of Architecture*.

* quoted in Timothy Ware, *The Orthodox Church*, (Penguin, 1991) p. 269.

How different that is from the simple chapel hut contained in my enclosure with its low table altar, open Bible, burning light before the icons – and yet that is also beautiful in its simple and homely way.

Old Testament worship had its altars and shrines, the tabernacle in the wilderness, its holy places and the Jerusalem temple. The early Church met in temple and synagogue, then in open places and hired halls and upper rooms. Prayer could be offered on a roof top with Peter, in a prison cell with Paul and Silas, or in the house of a believer where the church met for its liturgy.

When Jesus cried out: 'It is finished' and accomplished his sacrifice on the cross, the veil of the temple was torn from top to bottom, indicating that the way was now wide open into the very presence of God, for all believer-priests have access to the Father through him who is the Way, and by the power of the Holy Spirit.

Throughout the history of the Church, and in my own Franciscan Order, there have been those who have found a sense of God's presence much more real and accessible under the dome of the sky, on the mountain or in a verdant valley, than in a building with its ecclesiastical trappings which have sometimes served as obstacles to prayer and worship.

Of course it is possible to mingle both, in the blessing of the fields and land at Rogationtide, making the stations of the cross from tree to tree in Lent, or celebrating the Eucharist on the open-air altar in our Franciscan cemetery in Dorset. I remember a very moving Eucharist one early morning under the trees on the last day of the Merton retreat which I conducted. I certainly would not confine my worship, my repentance, my joy in God, to churches or religious services, for my sense of God's loving presence is stimulated anywhere and everywhere. Nevertheless, there are holy places, sanctified by holy people, holy events in the past, or hallowed by much prayer and loving worship. And I find it not only convenient, but necessary and precious to have a place set apart (holy means set apart), where I can worship, pray, meditate and wait upon God in silence.

WHAT KIND OF PLACE?

I have a hut, half of which is used for my bookbinding, icon mounting, and the making of prayer stools. The other half is dedicated to worship and prayer. It is perhaps too much to expect you to have a spare room (which is ideal), but you may have a small lumber-room, a space in the attic, or the corner of a quiet room where you can set up a prayer place for yourself, or for the family.

Of course, you can set up a small prayer hut in your garden, or a larger retreat hut which I describe in chapter six, but right now I shall assume that you have a corner of a quiet room. I shall describe my prayer place and you can adapt yours for your own needs.

Its basic use is for meditation and the saying of offices (morning and evening prayer, etc.). Also, there may be occasions when a house Eucharist is celebrated, so it would be helpful to be able to extend the area on such occasions, when a few people could gather.

First of all, clear the floor and wall area in the corner or along one wall of the room. Lay a piece of carpet to make kneeling or sitting easier, and provide a few cushions, and a prayer stool or firm chair.

Adapt a small, low table so that it is accessible from a kneeling position. Make and place two white linen coverings. On the altar table place a Bible open to the Gospel of the day, a candle or votive lamp and a small jar or vase of flowers. Obtain as large an icon as possible (perhaps one of the three mentioned in chapters eight to ten), and place it at the back of the altar table or hang it slightly above. A small cross or crucifix may be appropriate and incense is optional! Apart from the altar table it is useful to have a drawer or cupboard to keep stores in (extra candles, matches, incense, etc), and a shelf for liturgical and devotional books. On a nearby wall you could hang a map of the world, and reserve a place for the photographs of the people for whom you pray.

I will not list vessels for the Eucharist as I do not want to give the impression that this prayer place is a substitute for fellowship and worship around word and sacrament in your local church. You are not setting up a sect or conventicle!

If you do wish to deepen your life of prayer with a group of Christian friends, perhaps you should consider a retreat hut, the mysteries of which are revealed in the next chapter.

6

Furnishing a Hut for Retreats

WHY A HUT?

It's all very well my writing to you from a hermitage hut in the middle of the countryside and solitude, when you are surrounded by a busy job nursing in a city hospital, at the checkout of a supermarket, distracted by the demands of a young family, keeping on top of the latest business computer software, or even looking for work with the lassitude of that unemployed feeling. It is like a celibate monk or nun handing out advice on marital sexual compatibility!

Well it's not quite like that because I've been where you are. And in any case, you are already well into a book on the themes of prayer – one of the many busy people who are earnestly seeking an oasis of contemplative solitude because it has become a practical necessity – even a way to retain sanity. That is why a hut is a good idea, but before I develop it, let me tell you about five huts which have been significant to me.

When I went to Edinburgh to do some postgraduate study I lived for a year with the Community of the Transfiguration in Roslin, some miles outside the city. The community base consisted of a refurbished, corrugated, ex-village institute, with five or six huts in the enclosure garden. I have a note that my hut measured only 6' x 4', but surely it was bigger than that, though the brother in charge told me that the next smallest box I would inhabit would be my coffin!

Then up in the Pentland hills there was a retreat hut in an utterly solitary and beautiful place. Also the community had some huts in the hidden grounds of the small Cathedral of the Isles on the isle of Cumbrae on the west coast. When I wrote chapter three on setting up a hut hermitage for six months for Companions, I had this site in mind! The next hut in which I lived for six months was the 12' x 6' one which we erected in the fields adjoining the friary at Hilfield, Dorset, and that was the first real test of the solitary life.

My three years at Tymawr was spent in a small caravan which, although it was really too constricting, I feel a bit disloyal in saying so because it sheltered me in its welcoming and friendly feel for the whole of that time.

When I returned to Glasshampton in 1993 it was to a double hut hermitage and in such a context that I felt I was returning home to a hut spirituality. I don't know altogether why a hut is more appropriate than a caravan in which to test this kind of life. Perhaps it is because of its simplicity, its vulnerability, its lack of sophistication. Perhaps also, I associate caravans with beach parties and rowdy holiday camps, though I must admit that a caravan can be ideal in terms of its facilities and mobility. Yet I am so glad to be back in a hut.

Those early days in Roslin were very spartan. I remember waking up in the winter with a coating of frost where the condensation had frozen on my top blanket. My association with that hut-life is one of ascetic discipline, and a Celtic simplicity in the chapel hut where, in good Scottish Episcopal style the sacrament of the Eucharist and the sacrament of the word (an open Bible) were reserved together.

It was in those early huts that I learned the basic obedience to the disciplines of early rising, the recitation of the Psalter, hours of meditation in silence, and attendance upon the Gospel. I spent only one year with that community, but it gave me a thorough grounding in the gospel life, and in some ways was more Franciscan than my own present Franciscan Order. I remember now those early frosty mornings when I would hear Bishop Neil Russell's footsteps going past my hut to the chapel hut for meditation before 4.00 am each morning, summer days of prayer, walking and meditation around the still lake in the Pentland hills, and the periods in the Cumbrae community of huts, capturing the atmosphere of what some of the Celtic monastic communities may have been like.

A SHARED RETREAT HUT

I am not suggesting that everyone who wants to develop a life of prayer should furnish a prayer hut for retreats. There would be the problem of space, expense, and relevance to your particular prayer needs. What I am suggesting is that if you are not already linked up with a friendly family, a prayer group or a Third Order meeting, you should get together a few friends from your church community who are interested in developing their spiritual lives.

The idea would be that you would meet once a month around the general theme of spirituality with a reading list — perhaps taking it in turns to introduce or expound a particular chapter in your spiritual reading, at the same time sharing extracts from your own spiritual journal reflecting your own spiritual pilgrimage.

The 'centre' of such a meeting would be that one of the group would have spent two days and a night (at least) in the hut, as a kind of mini-retreat, and that the reading, study and experience written up in the spiritual journal should come from that retreat period.

The hut could be purchased by between four or six families, and all could share in the equipping of it. It would be erected in the most appropriate garden available, and it would not be used for holiday purposes but kept as a place of prayer and retreat for any member of the participating group, with an engagement diary for booking dates.

Even part of a day is useful in finding an oasis of quiet, but in order to carry out the monthly commitment, the retreatant should spend at least one night there, preferably two, for if you enter in on the first day, and emerge on the third, then you will have one whole day with no other concerns but God and yourself! From this period would come the report which you would write up and communicate to the monthly meeting. You need not be alarmed at such a commitment, for if there are six 'retreating' members, your turn would only come around every six months. In any case there would be no 'spiritual expectations' — it would rather be a sharing of 'how things were'.

One month a sister may report: 'Nothing extraordinary happened, but I did find myself unwinding and relaxed, so that I could walk and think, and even do some praying. I wasn't able to do much study, but I'll share what thoughts came to me on my evening walk as I went back to my childhood experience which had been lost to me over the years.'

Another month a brother may report: 'I had an awful time. I couldn't settle, I lacked concentration, and the weather didn't help. To be honest, I had no sense of God, but a real feeling of depression and of wasting time. I tried to read and couldn't, so I had beans on toast and slept most of the time.'

The next month might be: 'I went a bit fearfully, not knowing what to expect, and decided to go to sleep early because I was whacked. This meant that when I woke early for the whole day, I felt refreshed and had a warm sense of God's love, and a sort of quietness settled upon me, enabling me to write a lot in my journal, though I didn't do much reading.'

Some may return shining with renewed vision, while others may feel a deep sense of their own inadequacy and failure, with all variations between. It is *all* grist to your mill. As a group you will find a brother experiencing and carrying *your* burden, pain and anxieties, or a sister catching a glimpse of *your* hope, glory and hidden longing. Nothing is lost, for you will be finding, individually and together, the presence of God in the light and shadow of prayer in solitude and sharing it with the others. You may well find that for the first time you will feel another's joys and pains most intimately, and the gifts of wisdom and discernment for one another will show your corporate concern and growth in prayer.

There is also the added bonus of all of you having a few days — for where there are children they could be 'shared' with the other families in the group, and the children may well enjoy a holiday from mum and dad.

As well as personal journals, it may be profitable to have a communal journal in which any of the members would be free to write his or her contribution, on a regular basis. The value of recording experiences is that you will be able to see a pattern emerging over a period, and realize that growth is taking place, that you have proved God in times of dryness, aridity and trial, and enjoyed God at times when, for no apparent reason, he has invaded your soul with grace and joy, imparting the ability to meditate and intercede in new and productive ways.

There will be times of boredom, tedium and even desolation, but there will also be experiences of enlightenment, discernment and sheer joy. These will sometimes be personal and sometimes corporate, for the group will vary in changes of mood and temperament, as well as the individual. The desert fathers sometimes spoke of the hut or cell as the antechamber of heaven, but sometimes as the furnace in which Shadrach, Meshach and Abednego were cast. We may be consoled by the fact that the searing, fiery judgment of God is also the purging fire of divine Love which consumes our dross and refines the gold to reflect his image within us, to his glory.

PRACTICAL LAYOUT

If you live in a hut for any length of time, you have to learn to be practical, clean and methodical, for a spirituality which is not earthed is not likely to be effective in either the spiritual or the material world. I'll describe my living hut, and you will get the idea of your needs so that you can add or subtract to my list as you get acquainted with hut life.

I purchased my 12' x 8' living hut in Kidderminster, at the same time buying a 4' x 4' loo and toolshed hut. For a small extra cost the dealers will erect the hut/s for you, but you will need to have prepared either a concrete apron the right size or at least a level foundation of railway sleepers or breeze blocks. It is as well to have it 'dipped' before delivery, and you can keep it weatherproofed as part of your manual work. Make sure you have an opening window, and you'll need curtain rails and curtains made, with perhaps a curtain on the inside of the door.

You should line the hut with hardboard or compressed board, filling the space with fibreglass insulation. Paint the inside white and fix some bookshelves and cup hooks. Also make a small wooden frame to hold a plastic bowl and draining board with shelves beneath to store crockery, cutlery, etc., covered by a curtain.

Then hardboard the floor and carpet it. The carpet sample squares (underneath) and the covering carpet were given me for the hermitage by friends at one of the Kidderminster carpet companies.

I prefer my iron hospital bed, for it has space underneath for storage. You'll need a small sturdy table and upright chair for work, and a small easy chair. A chest of drawers would be very helpful, and another small table to house a butane cooker (cylinder beneath). If you have a power line you could have a baby electric cooker with a socket also for a lamp and heater. If not, then have a butane or propane heater and good paraffin lamp (or candles) for light.

Learn from me that butane (blue) cylinders freeze below nought degrees centigrade, but propane (orange) cylinders do not. Also condensation can be a real problem with cylinder gas, so get a power line if possible, for dry heat. My gas cooker has two rings, a grill and small oven – it is good to make your own bread! Incidental pieces like crockery, cutlery, containers and linen I leave to you, but I find two good well-lidded plastic bins are excellent for perishables and keep mice away. Don't forget to fix guttering on your hut and a rain butt, and you'll need an Elsan toilet and spade for disposal (I said you need to be earthed)!

I have a chapel and workhut now, but formerly everything had to be in one place, so I set up a worship area in one corner, – you'll find a description of such a place in chapter five, so I won't repeat it here. It may be a good idea to lay exterior paving stones too, for when there is rain and thick mud outside it is good to be clean and snug inside.

When you have set all this up, without making a big fuss (for it is meant to be a hidden place of prayer), you may like to ask your priest or pastor to lead a dedication or blessing ceremony along the lines described in chapter two. It would be too small to celebrate the Eucharist for the whole group, unless you arranged a house Eucharist and processed down to the hut for the blessing, or celebrated an open-air Eucharist in the garden.

You will find that there will grow up a common, mutual and pastoral responsibility in the group for one another and for the hut. I am presuming that members of the group will be living a sacramental and gospel life from their own local church, and though the hut will be hidden, it must not be an alternative to corporate church life. You will be amazed at what may grow out of such an experiment, for apart from influencing others to set up a similar cell, it may be that a vocation will develop within the group to the kind of amazing hermit life that is undergoing a revival in the Church at this present time.

So now the place is ready – either a quiet corner in your home or a hut. But what about *you*? That can be dealt with in the next chapter, which provides a simple method of biblical meditation.

7

A Method of Meditation

SIMPLICITY

There is an increasing volume of writing and teaching about meditation and retreats, with workshops galore in the Christian and wider religious world. Meditation is popular, and methods, schemes and techniques abound. I have taught and written much about the practice of meditation and have been surrounded by so much spoken and written teaching, so it is refreshing to find, at the beginning of *The Inner Christ* by John Main (Darton, Longman and Todd, 1987), just one single paragraph as follows:

How to Meditate

Sit down. Sit still and upright. Close your eyes lightly. Sit relaxed but alert. Silently, interiorly begin to say a single word. We recommend the prayer-phrase 'maranatha'. Recite it as four syllables of equal length. Listen to it as you say it, gently but continuously. Do not think or imagine anything – spiritual or otherwise. If thoughts and images come, these are distractions at the time of meditation, so keep returning to simply saying the word. Meditate each morning and evening for between twenty and thirty minutes.

The good thing about such simplicity is that it says 'this is it – now get on with it,' and from actually doing it, consistent and habitually twice a day, you will learn from your joys and mistakes the way to go forward.

Of course, the book then goes on for well over 300 pages to expound, delineate, teach, suggest, correct and commend all sorts of material related to meditation, and a whole compendium of excellent counsel stems from the meditative repetition of that one word 'maranatha'. The meditator can also join one of the many meditation groups which meet across the country under the care of the Christian Meditation Centre based in London (it is also world-wide).

Meditation is indeed a simple matter, and there are certain people who are able, from childhood, to sit in a relaxed posture, breathe gently, deeply, rhythmically, who begin with Scripture, theme or story before them, and move through reading and meditation into silence and ever-deepening contemplation. It is natural, basic and simple.

The problem is that such people are rare. It is not meditation that is complicated – but we ourselves. We need to unlearn our wrong practices, withdraw from our frenetic activities, still our twitching, tense bodies, and let go our harassing, distressing, anxious and distracting thoughts. And that is not simple or easy. The paradox is that we know it is not easy because we are complicated, yet we must affirm that it is *meant* to be easy. It is our natural birthright as human beings, and we see it reflected in the relaxed and abandoned posture of a baby, of an animal at rest, and in the world of nature when the trees are gently letting go their leaves (as they are today outside my window) and the sap descends for the period of rest, preparation and waiting.

SETTING ABOUT IT

As you read this kind of a book, you are likely to be well aware that things are not simple, and that you are a mass of contradictions and complications. Yet also there will be the knowledge that your mind and heart have been touched and moved by the need and longing for prayer and meditation, so some plain and practical explanation of method is called for.

You are also persuaded that prayer is an inspired movement within the heart and a discipline to be integrated into the wholeness of your daily life. If there is no fire then there will be no light or heat, and if there is no discipline then the ignited coals will soon burn themselves out. But presuming that there is a living flame on the altar of your heart, how do you tend it, nurture and sustain it?

I use the word *meditation* to indicate the kind of prayer that feeds upon the fuel of Scripture, symbol/theme from the natural world or the *Jesus Prayer*, with a linking of the mind and heart — what the Orthodox would describe as the 'mind descending to the heart'. But the vistas of contemplative prayer move on far beyond this. When I use the word *contemplation* I indicate a further stage or deepening in which the believer is not thinking or imagining but simply *being* in the enveloping and indwelling presence of God — beyond thought, logic, image — but simply in love. This is the goal of all prayer and meditation, for it is here that you are drawn into that divine circular communion of love which is portrayed in Rublev's icon of the Holy Trinity.

From those soaring heights of spiritual experience let me be practical and show you the way in. Look at the following meditation schemes:

73

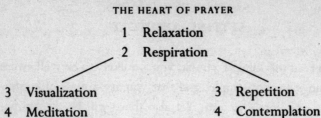

1 Relaxation
2 Respiration

3 Visualization   3 Repetition
4 Meditation   4 Contemplation
5 Contemplation

The scheme on the left applies to the kind of meditation which involves praying with Scripture, a devotional theme or a symbol from the natural world (e.g. a candle, a tree, music). The scheme on the right applies to the simple and continuous repetition of a word, a Scripture verse or the *Jesus Prayer* in which the repetition begins on the lips, moves to the mind and descends to the heart. Both these schemes lead to a measure of contemplative prayer, and the dimension of contemplation is infinitely wide and deep. Both schemes begin similarly, and the right-hand scheme is found in John Main's meditation teaching or in the chapter on the *Jesus Prayer* in this book. So let me open up the left-hand scheme, illustrating it with an actual meditation from Scripture which I have used with many groups in teaching meditative prayer.

1 Relaxation. Meditation is a work as well as an art, and setting about it requires a suitable place. This may be the corner of a church or oratory, a quiet room, a hut, an open field or garden, or some bolt hole where you can get away from disturbance. It is best to avoid tight clothing, a track or leisure suit is best, and no footwear.

Then you need to relax your body. It means first finding the right posture – which may be sitting on a stool or upright chair, kneeling with a prayer stool, sitting in a cross-legged or lotus posture or lying on your back or tummy (if not too soporific). I choose a prayer stool.

Then the simple process of relaxation can be practised. Basically it means beginning with the soles of the feet and progressing up to the crown of the head, stretching and relaxing, telling each part of your body to let go and rest. It is worth getting advice and doing some relaxation exercises with a group or guide. When the body is relaxed but alert, and the back is straight, then attention must be given to breathing.

2 Respiration. The second step is the opening of the human spirit to the Holy Spirit. You give attention to your breathing – your own respiration, and to the breathing of the Spirit of God who dwells within you. In terms of respiration, it is a good practice to learn to breathe from the diaphragm rather than from the top of the chest – belly breathing instead of shallow chest breathing. Slow, deep, rhythmic breathing – but with no push or strain. Everything should be easy – easy come, easy go. Continue breathing like this for a minute or two until you find your own gentle rhythm. At this point, people who practise the John Main method or the *Jesus Prayer* either begin to say the prayer according to their breathing rhythm, or they become aware of their heart beat and repeat the prayer according to that measure. The word *inspiration* also indicates the breathing of the Holy Spirit within the human spirit – thus the prayer 'Breathe on me, Breath of God'.

3 Visualization. There are many forms of imaginative prayer, dream and vision both inside and outside the biblical pages. If we have opened our minds and hearts to the inspiration of the Holy Spirit and have the word of Scripture before us, then we shall be guided by the text into a meditative understanding. We shall be carried into the Scripture's plain meaning, into the implications of its teaching and into a personal or group application of its meaning for our day, for our lives and for our present situation.

Visualization begins with the actual reading of the selected text and the opening up of the text's meaning as the Holy Spirit stimulates the imaginative faculties. In this step it is the mind of the meditator which is at work, co-operating with the Holy Spirit, and this leads on to the next step which is the offering up of your heart and mind to the Spirit's illumination.

4 Meditation. The fourth step begins the actual meditation as the believer is carried into the pages of the Bible, actually participating in the situation described in the text. You begin by an objective evaluation of the scene, and then allow yourself to be ever more deeply drawn into the activity and movement of the story, parable, miracle or whatever passage is being studied. This is an imaginative meditation by experience, so that you identify with Abraham being called out from Ur of the Chaldees, Isaac walking to sacrifice with his father on Mount Moriah, Jacob running away in the wilderness from Esau, Samuel the child as he hears God calling to him in the darkness, or with Jeremiah or the Psalmist lying in a well or pit of despair. In the New Testament, the Gospels and the Acts of the Apostles are full of situations which may become relevant to your own pilgrimage and vocation. As well as giving clear ethical and doctrinal teaching, they are full of principles of action which impinge on our own lives.

We make Scripture our own by such imaginative and prayerful meditation in its pages, so that the characters of the Bible become our friends, and their lives intertwine with ours in the pilgrimage of faith. When St Paul spoke of the journey of the Israelites in the wilderness he clearly meant that their journey should become ours and that we should identify with their pilgrimage in the avoiding of sins and the following of our heavenly Moses in the journey from earth to heaven (e.g. 1 Corinthians 10:1–13). The writer of the Hebrew letter certainly meant us to identify with the heroes of faith so that we may enter into their experience and emulate their faith and victory (see Hebrews ch. 11 throughout), and he concludes:

> Therefore, since we are surrounded by so great a cloud of witnesses, let us also lay aside every weight and the sin that clings so closely, and let us run with perseverance the race that is set before us, looking to Jesus the pioneer and perfecter of our faith . . .

Ultimately we meditate and participate *with* Jesus in the words and works of his ministry on earth and then identify *in* Jesus as he enters into the pain and sorrows of Calvary and death, and rises to glory and newness of life. Such identification is the root and sap of Christian mystical theology, exemplified by St Paul in words which would be amazing if they were not so familiar:

> I have been crucified with Christ, and it is no longer I who live, but it is Christ who lives in me. And the life I now live in the flesh I live by faith in the Son of God who loved me and gave himself for me. (Galatians 2:20).

5 Contemplation. This word includes a wide spectrum of experience and attitude, from a simple sense of wonder at the beauty and power of Jesus speaking, healing, dying and rising in the pages of the Gospels to the timeless adoration of eternal union with God which is beyond language and understanding in this life. It is the endless, adoring wonder of those who are caught up into the very being of God in his eternal Trinitarian life of glory and love – the consummation of all things in which rests the stillness and the dynamic of all creation.

We are considering here only the beginnings of such contemplation – the upper reaches of meditation as it were. But if we embark upon the meditative reading and praying of Scripture we shall certainly glimpse something of the eternal glory of God in Jesus, by the power of the Holy Spirit. If we join company with the seers, prophets, apostles and with Jesus himself, we shall be struck down with the wonder and majesty of God, we shall be melted by his love and transfigured by his glory. Isaiah cried out in mortal and spiritual agony at the vision of God; Ezekiel fell on his face before God's glory, and Daniel felt all his strength drain away before the vision. At one point Peter looked upon the face of Jesus and said: 'Depart from me, for I am a sinful man, O Lord.' And when the three disciples entered into the cloud of glory on Tabor, they became speechless with adoring wonder.

I have been consciously following the way of Jesus since I was twelve years of age (and unconsciously from my infancy), and some of the most precious and revelatory moments of my life have been the experiences of God within the pages of holy Scripture. I have laughed and I have wept; I have danced and I have lain smitten on the ground; I have proclaimed with great assurance and been struck with silence – all because of the power of the Holy Spirit within my heart through the word of Scripture. And I can translate that last sentence quite easily into the present tense, for it happens now – it happens today, as I hear and understand, and give my mind and heart to obedience and love. All this comes from meditation and the beginnings of contemplation, for out of the experience of adoring wonder there is the overflow of a life given to God in words and works of love. Meditative contemplation means to love God with all your heart, soul, mind and strength, and to love your neighbour – including friend and enemy – in the reconciling Gospel of Jesus. Come now then and follow me in the actual meditation itself.

LETTING IT HAPPEN

My Bible is open at St Mark 5:24–34 – the healing of the woman with the chronic haemorrhage. First of all I find my quiet place, with a candle burning before the icon. I wear loose clothing with no footwear. I sit on my prayer stool, with straight back and no strain, allowing any stress and 'up tightness' to flow away in the relaxing atmosphere of the loving presence of God. I allow a minute or two for settling down, then gently begin to practise the relaxation technique of stretching and relaxing from the soles of my feet to the crown of my head. Then gently I allow my breathing to slow down, and become aware of the Holy Spirit, the breath of God, breathing in and through me.

Now, when I find myself outwardly and inwardly quiet, I

take up the text and read it right through, not hurriedly, but not yet dwelling on any particular words or phrases, in order to set the scene and be surrounded by the atmosphere of the story.

So I arrive at the place where I read the text again – but this time slowly and imaginatively, waiting, watching, enquiring – moving from one part of the scene to another, or quietly observing various characters in their interaction and movement. Sometimes this is the most fruitful part of the meditation because the words and phrases allow my participation as I move progressively through the text. At other times I allow the text to minister to me, closing my eyes and allowing the story to unfold in imaginative vision, and I am borne along in the meditation by the Spirit's interior movement.

On this occasion I find myself carried into the text as I read it and feel it drawing out of me my own feelings of curiosity, perplexity, emptiness, weariness, hope, anticipation and growing wonder and faith in Jesus the healer.

THE MEDITATION

I find myself gently being let down in the midst of a great crowd. I am unnoticed because in the shove and push of the crowd we are all trying to move along with Jesus who is on his way to lay hands on a dying girl, daughter of Jairus, an elder of the synagogue.

It's a hot day and I can feel the dust between the toes of my sandalled feet – I can hear and see and even smell the crowd thronging and moving along. I'm looking for someone, and at last I see her. I know a bit about her from the text, and as I

80

watch her unobserved, I can see and then feel all her pain and desperation. As I try to enter into the depths of her feelings and understand her longings, I begin to feel myself thinking through her mind, feeling from her heart, longing with her faith.

How long it has been – fully twelve years of weariness and pain, of chronic bleeding, of religious and social rejection. The nature of her disease means that she cannot worship with the people of God or mix freely with any social group. All the money she possessed has long ago been spent on physicians and medicines – all to no avail. She has come to the end of her tether.

Now I can feel the debilitating anxiety, the fear and trembling that takes hold of her as she is moved by the crowd, edging forward toward Jesus. 'If only I can touch him,' is the dominant thought in her mind. There is nothing else to do now, nowhere else to go, no one else to trust – only him. If only . . . All the weariness of twelve long years of sickness and pain, of loneliness and isolation, of fears and rejection, are gathered up in her determination, and all the longing, the hope, the mingled faith and desire which Jesus draws out of her.

Now see her within a stone's throw of him . . . edging, pushing, elbowing nearer. And then, suddenly . . . reaching out . . . touching . . . believing . . . and suddenly – suddenly being shot through with energy, strength, power and healing!

Alleluia!
It's done!
In a moment!
* Wholeness *
Alleluia!

81

The whole world has changed – radiance, healing, physical well-being – and joy! In that one, glorious moment it seems as if the world stands still, the crowd is silenced – there is only Jesus and her! Alleluia!

And then. A word from heaven. 'Who touched me?' Jesus is looking around – of course he knows, for as she felt power enter into her, he felt power leaving him. And she knows. And she knows that he knows, and he knows that she knows! There's no one else in the world – but she trembles now with a new fear – and yet also vibrant with faith.

Listen to the disciples, irritated and perplexed under the afternoon sun. 'Lord,' says Peter, 'everyone is touching you, look at the crowd – what do you mean?' But she knows, and she comes and falls down before him, and tells her story – and out it all comes. She tells of the years of pain and weariness, the longing, the uncleanness, the social rejection, the religious isolation, the sheer emptiness of her soul. Her tears are a mingling of sorrow and joy now, and her sadness mingles with his compassion, and again there is no one else in the world, but Jesus only . . . 'My daughter,' he says, (and his words are like the sound of many waters), 'your faith has made you whole. Go in peace and be free from all your suffering . . .' And the world turns over in love.

These are my tears – this is my joy – and so it all comes back to me. I need you now, Lord, I feel the compassion and healing power flowing through you, and I feel my own bankruptcy and weariness. I am carried deeper and deeper into the healing power of Jesus, by the life-giving dynamism of the Spirit, down into the mystery of the love of God. And on . . . on to contemplation . . .

RETURN TO SIMPLICITY

At this point I cannot say more, for it is the work of the
Holy Spirit to carry you deeper into contemplative prayer.
Sometimes the period will end here, with thanksgiving and a
gentle 'coming out' of the meditation period in quietness, back
into the world of activity and relationships, but with a new
radiance and vitality. But sometimes there will be a moving
onward, forward, higher and deeper into the mystery of
prayer. And if you want to know more about that, enquire
further into the great mystical tradition, your heart filled with
the insights of scripture.

What began as a commendation of the simplicity of meditation has turned out to be some detailed methodological guidance, but I return to the matter of simplicity. It is that you sit
quietly before God, calling upon his Spirit to lead you to know
him and to love him . . . and that is the beginning of a fruitful
contemplative way.

Vladimir Iconostasis

8

Meditation Before an Icon

It must have been twenty years ago when I attended the annual conference of the Anglican-Orthodox *Fellowship of St Andrew and St Sergius*. I was moved with wonder at the simplicity and power of one of the sessions. A very large reproduction of Andrei Rublev's icon of *The Old Testament Trinity* (*Philoxenia*) was set before us, and Militza Zernov stood beside it and led us into a meditative exposition of the beauty and teaching of the icon.

She personified the teaching that an icon is a window into the divine revelation of God, and that honour and worship is not accorded to the material icon but *through* the icon to God alone. St John of Damascus affirms the wonder of the Incarnation by making the point:

I do not adore matter, but I adore the Creator of matter, who became matter for me, inhabiting matter and accomplishing my salvation through matter.

The word *icon* comes from the Greek *eikon* meaning image, and the word occurs in the Septuagint reading of Genesis 1:27: 'So God created humankind in his image.' It refers to Christ in Colossians 1:15: 'He is the image of the invisible God.' Christ uniquely and perfectly bears the image of the Father, and we are meant to reflect that image in holiness and love. The icon is a window into eternity in that, in a humble and material way, it reflects something of the divine mystery, the sublime love, of God made manifest to his creatures.

An icon is a representation of Christ or the saints in the Orthodox tradition, and is not an end in itself, but a means to an end. It is an aid to devotion and its true end or purpose is the offering of adoration and prayer to God. As a window, you may look *upon* the icon, and then *through* the icon, in the manner of George Herbert's lines:

> A man that looks on glass
> on it may stay his eye;
> or if he pleases, through it pass,
> and then the heaven espy.

What the Bible does in words, the icon shows forth in form, colour and visual beauty. It is not intellectual or cerebral, but intuitive in its communication, so that the mind may descend into the heart, and that holiness, love, mystery and compassion may be felt and understood at an affective level, thus evoking adoration, tenderness and the worship of the whole person.

What has happened during the last few decades is that the Western Church has been profoundly influenced by the Orthodox icons of the Eastern Church, so that they are found not only in the monastic houses of the Anglican and Roman Catholic communions, but in the Reformed community of Taizé, France, and in many parish churches in our own country.

It is not my intention to give a history of iconography,* but simply to set down meditations on three of the most famous icons in order to initiate and stimulate your interest, and enable you to contemplate the glory and wonder of God as you sit before an icon in that place of the heart which is the space between the icon and the believer.

Militza Zernov described what happened when the over-painted and darkened icon of Rublev reached its final stage of restoration — and this description may be a symbol of what may happen in your heart as you contemplate the glory of the living God:

> *The restoration of the icon of the Holy Trinity took several years, from 1904 until 1919. The metal adornment and up to eight layers of consecutive repainting were removed. There is a dramatic account of an eye witness of how the last layer disappeared. The icon was flooded with alcohol, which was set on fire, burning the dry crust, and as by a miracle, the original icon appeared in its astonishing beauty.*

What happens when you sit quietly, in recollection and gentle mindfulness before an icon, with your heart open to the Holy Spirit, depends on the loving sovereignty of God. The content of your meditation may take a quite different direction from the three meditations I share with you here, but certainly that 'window into eternity' will allow light, truth and love to shine into your heart, dispelling ignorance and

---

* A readily accessible book on icons by an Anglican priest is recommended: John Baggley, *Doors of Perception*, (London: Mowbray, 1987).

gloom and illuminating both heart and mind in true adoration.

THE OLD TESTAMENT TRINITY
BY ANDREI RUBLEV, C. 1411

I sit on my prayer stool before what has been called the 'icon of
icons'. The light of the candle flickers before the three angels of
Genesis 18:1–15, and the Greek title *philoxenia* meaning hos-
pitality, is the context in which Rublev represents the Holy
Trinity. He does away with the characters and details found in
other Trinity icons, so that the divine circle of love is open to
the believer, and draws me into a participation in the Trinitarian
life which flows between the persons of the Holy Trinity.

There are some details in the background, but they do not
intrude into the circle of love. The building on the top left
indicates the Church of God, and it is typical of Orthodox
Spirituality that important as the Church is, it is God in his
Trinitarian glory who is central. The Church must not pro-
claim itself, but the redeeming love of God in Christ.

The central tree in the background represents the oak of
mamre in the Genesis account and symbolizes the Tree of Life
which, though out of bounds in fallen Eden, is now accessible
in the paradise of God. The mountain rising in the top right is
the symbol of the presence of God communicating with his
people from the high and sacred place.

My attention is drawn back to the centre. I recall how an
ancient manuscript reports:

On feast days, Andrei together with his friend the icon painter and companion, with whom he fasted, did not paint but sat in front of the divine icons, contemplating them without ceasing: they were filled with joy, their minds being lifted towards uncreated Divine Light.

The three winged angels become the image of the triune God, and they all hold equal sceptres of power and are in profound communion around the eucharistic chalice of sacrificial love. The chalice contained grapes in an overpainting, but under it was found the figure of a lamb – the lamb slain before the foundation of the world (Revelation 33:8).

There are two schools of thought within Orthodoxy as to which figure represents which person of the Trinity and we are reminded that they are not portraits, but symbolic representations. I recall the interpretation which Militza Zernov expounded.

The three persons share the divine nature represented in the garment of blue, the colour of heaven, for it is one divine life and being which is manifested in the *hypostases*, or persons, of the Holy Trinity. The garments of the central angel stand in bold contrast with the whiteness of the altar table, the figure representing God the Father, who is the fountainhead or source of the Holy Trinity. I am attracted to the mystery and wonder of this figure, for as Melitza says: 'It is like a fountain from which everything else in the icon springs, but a silent fountain.'

The Father reveals himself through the Son and the Spirit, which are 'the two hands' of the Father, and he gazes upon the Son in benediction, making the sign of blessing upon the chalice of suffering.

The Son, on the left, lifts his eyes slightly in consent and obedience, his right hand resting on his knee. He reciprocates the gesture of the Father's benediction, the two fingers indicating the two natures of Christ in the Orthodox priestly blessing. He wears the brown robe of humanity covering the blue robe of divinity, but the brown garment is partly transparent so that the divinity of Christ shines through his humanity.

The figure on the right represents the Holy Spirit who receives the contemplative gaze of the Son and reflects it toward the Father. It is strangely beautiful that the three faces are one, and the three haloes are radiant with the one light. The third figure is the bond of union between the Father and the Son, and as John of Damascus said, it is by the Holy Spirit that we know Christ the Son of God, and by the Son we contemplate the Father. As well as the blue of divinity the third figure wears the green of fertility, because, according to the Nicene creed, he is the Lord, the giver of life. And as the symbol of the living Church rises behind the Christ, so the mountain of revelation rises behind the Spirit, reminding us of the sacred heights of Sinai and Carmel, of Tabor, Hermon and the Mount of Olives. 'The Old Testament,' says St Gregory Nazianzen, 'manifested the Father plainly, the Son obscurely. The New Testament revealed the Son and hinted at the divinity of the Holy Spirit. Today the Spirit dwells among us and makes himself more clearly known.'

Gazing upon this beautiful icon I hear echoing and re-echoing within my heart: 'The Father loves the Son, loves the Spirit . . . the Son loves the Spirit, loves the Father . . . the Spirit loves the Father, loves the Son.'

I am drawn into this communion of love, this sharing in the very life of God, for I am a creature made in the image (icon) of God, and I have been redeemed by the cleansing of Christ's blood and by the sanctification of the Holy Spirit.

Here, in this icon, is manifested profound meditation, tranquillity, and peace. And yet there is the potential dynamic of creation and redemption – all within the mystery and beauty of God – Father, Son and Holy Spirit.

9

Icon: Our Lady of Vladimir

THEOTOKOS (GOD BEARER ICONS)

When I settled into my present hermitage, Michael made me a simple, but beautiful *iconostasis* to house the large reproduction of Our Lady of Vladimir icon. The original was painted in Constantinople about 1130 and went to Russia as part of the Orthodox Faith. It is my favourite of the Theotokos (God bearer icon) of which there are different types.

There is the *Orans* gesture, where Mary appears as the image of the Church, with arms raised in prayer, often the half figure of Christ suspended in an aureole in front of Mary's breast. This 'Immanuel' figure gives a blessing with his right hand and holds the scroll of Isaiah 7:14 in his left: 'Therefore the Lord himself shall give you a sign; behold a virgin shall conceive and bear a son, and shall call his name Immanuel.' (AV). Therefore, this icon is called 'Mother of God of the Sign'.

Another type is the *Hodigitria* (Pointer of the Way), where Mary is portrayed in solemnity, the child enthroned upon her left arm, while her right hand points to Christ as Redeemer. One of the most beautiful of these icons is *The Smolensk Mother of God*, painted in the sixteenth century. In this type of icon, tenderness gives way to solemnity. The child is small, but more than an infant, portraying the pre-eternal God with divine authority to bless and to teach, with benediction and scroll. Mary enthrones the incarnate Son and gazes upon him in contemplative inwardness.

Our Lady of Vladimir icon is of the *Eleusa* (Mother of Mercy) type, not bearing the Byzantine severity of the *Hodigitria*, but emphasizing the maternal, tender, compassionate and sorrowing aspects of Mary, cradling the Christ child on her right arm, while he is depicted with one hand lovingly around his mother's neck, while the other grasps her *maphorian* (outer garment).

There is also a mixture of these two latter types called the *Glykophilusa* (Mother of Tenderness), but these are found rather in Italy and Crete than Russia. We turn then to *Our Lady of Vladimir*.

MEDITATION

In the stillness of the reflecting light and shadows of candle flame I look upon this icon, understanding why it is found in so many Orthodox homes with a light burning before it. 'You are welcome, Mary,' cry the children, while the relatives pray for a loved one saying: 'Do not remove your mercy, do not hide your charity, pure Virgin Mary, but lead me now and remember me in the hour of judgment.'

I look into the eyes of Our Lady and am moved by the tenderness towards her child, the prophetic pain and sorrow of his dying, the compassion for all the world's sadness. She bears the sorrow of the Russian soul within her, and all the struggle and conflict of decades of martyrdom. She bears it patiently, lovingly, and victoriously.

See the manner in which the Christ child embraces her, pressing his cheek to hers, his heart to hers, his hands entwined lovingly around her. The whole attitude of the Christ child is one of simplicity. The way in which his small feet are extended, exposing the sole of his left foot, expresses the vulnerability of God become a child; I am reminded of the lines of Charles Wesley:

My God, contracted to a span,
Incomprehensibly made man!

This particular icon reveals the strong tendency in Orthodoxy not to portray the Mother without the child, for she is because of him, and he is her Saviour and God. Also, although prayers and devotion are offered to Our Lady, it is only 'in Christ' that this is done. She prays for us as our Mother (John 19:27), and we humbly ask her to pray for us to her Son and Saviour.

See the way in which Mary's arm supports her little Son, her hands caress him, her tenderness unites them both in one movement of love. Thinking upon the affective and gentle sorrow of Mary before me, I reflect upon the prophecy of Simeon when holding the child in his arms, he prophesied: '. . . a sword shall pierce your own soul too.' Again, when the boy Jesus was found in the temple after days of searching, he answered Mary with words of wisdom, and 'his mother treasured all these things in her heart.' And I stand with Mary at the cross of her dear, suffering Son. Her heart was nailed there with him, and her tears mingled with his precious blood:

Who on Christ's dear Mother gazing,
In her trouble so amazing,
Born of woman, would not weep?
Who on Christ's dear Mother thinking,
Such a cup of sorrow drinking,
Would not share her sorrow deep?

I kneel here before this beautiful icon of *Our Lady of Vladimir*, and I join my prayers, my sorrows, my tears, with hers, while the arms of Christ enfold us both in the divine embrace . . . and we are loved . . .

10

Icon: The Christ Pantocrator

PANTOCRATOR: THE ALL-RULING CHRIST

If the *Vladimir* icon of Mary Theotokos (God bearer) carries the gentle child Christ as God made man in the Incarnation, so the *Pantocrator* icon depicts the sovereignty of the cosmic Christ who has conquered the powers of darkness and evil and brought all kingdoms and dominions under the rule of his love:

> *Holy, holy, holy,*
> *the Lord God the Almighty (Pantocrator),*
> *who was and is and is to come.*
> *(Revelation 4:8)*

He is the Alpha and Omega, the source and end of the Church's life and adoration (Revelation 5:12–14; 11:15–17).

In many Orthodox churches the *Pantocrator* is portrayed in the top part of the dome, sometimes with Mary Theotokos and John the Baptist. Beneath the *Pantocrator*, in the drum of the dome are the prophets, and below them the four evangelists, and descending into the body of the church the twelve major feasts and scenes from the Gospels, then at the lowest level the frescoes of the great saints of the Church triumphant and militant on earth. John Baggley writes of the design:

> The earthly church is the recipient of revelation from the Pantocrator mediated through the prophets, evangelists, and teachers of previous generations; it receives inspiration from the contemplation of the earthly life of Christ; and it engages in prayer and worship in union with the saints and the whole Mystical Body of Christ.*

In many of these *Pantocrator* icons, Christ's right hand is raised in blessing, sometimes turned towards his heart, indicating the inner knowledge and love that is expressed in the book or scroll in his left hand. The text often written in the book is Matthew 11:28,30:

> Come to me all you that are weary and are carrying heavy burdens, and I will give you rest . . . For my yoke is easy, and my burden is light.

From my first experiment of six months' solitude in 1982 I have always carried a remarkable *Pantocrator* icon which comes from Chevtogne, bearing the traditional letters IC XC (Jesus Christ), and the Greek letters for 'The One' in the halo, emphasizing Christ's cosmic role rather than the Incarnation. Yet this icon bears an expression of holiness mingled with mercy, and it always communicates the burning love of Christ which fills me with tenderness and awe. I keep it now in my

---

* *Doors of Perception*, (op.cit.) p. 91.

living hut, and it is the one before which I spend the present dark hours of early morning meditation.

PREPARATION

My meditation today is before the *Pantocrator* icon, and I practise a form of prayer which opens up my whole being to Christ, seeking his renewal and healing and energizing power. It is a method of prayer which I would commend to you when you feel physically weak, mentally tired, ignorant, or spiritually cast down.

In this icon, the halo surrounding Christ's head is particularly radiant, the breath of Christ, which is the Holy Spirit, surrounds me as I meditate, and the gesture of Christ's blessing is toward his heart of love.

The meditation is therefore threefold, asking that light from the *mind* of Christ may shine into my mind, that life from the *breath* of Christ may breathe into my body, and that love from the *heart* of Christ may be kindled in my heart. The appropriate Scriptures are:

1 *Let the same mind be in you that was in Christ Jesus*
(Philippians 2:5)
2 *He breathed on them and said: 'Receive the Holy Spirit'*
(John 20:22)
3 *Learn from Me, for I am gentle and humble in heart*
(Matthew 11:29)

As I pray and meditate, it is not only an offering of adoration, but a dwelling within the presence of Christ so that his healing, blessing and grace may be reproduced in me. Clarity for the *mind*, healing for the *body*, and fire for the *spirit*. There is a reciprocal relation between myself and Christ, and the result of such meditation will be that the compassion and joy of my Lord will spill over into my daily life, affecting those around me. So come with me as we put all this into practice.

MEDITATION

My meditation place is quiet and welcoming, with the open Bible and the flickering candle burning before the icon of Christ Pantocrator. As I sit on my prayer stool I am already relaxed, my breathing slow and rhythmic, and my attention is directed towards the icon . . . I make the invocation: 'In the name of the Father, and of the Son, and of the Holy Spirit. Amen.'

Now, when I feel ready, I begin to repeat the threefold prayer verbally for as long as it seems appropriate (from twenty to a hundred times), until the lips become silent, and the prayer continues in mind and heart:

Light from the mind of Christ, illumine me;
Life from the breath of Christ, enliven me;
Love from the heart of Christ, inflame me.

That's all it is, simply sitting, watching, listening, repeating, and waiting upon the Lord in the stillness.

CONTEMPLATION

If *meditation* is something which I undertake towards God, then *contemplation* is what the Holy Spirit accomplishes within me. I can prepare for it, long for it, be open to it and co-operate with it, but only God can initiate and sustain it within me. As I wait in his presence, meditating before the icon, repeating my prayer and trusting in his word, then I can expect God to do his own work in his own time.

There will be occasions when I am full of joy and sweetness; others when I will have to pray in faith with no emotional 'high'; and there may be times when I feel myself in the land of unknowing, aridity and darkness. No matter. The important thing is that I remain there, affirming the loving presence of God, whether I can *feel* it or not; that is *his* business.

But if I undertake this discipline of prayer regularly, then spontaneity will eventually follow, and the will of God will be accomplished in my life – and in yours!

Lord Jesus Christ,
Son of God,
have mercy on me,
a sinner

Orthodox Prayer Rope

11

The Jesus Prayer

**LORD JESUS CHRIST * SON OF GOD
* HAVE MERCY ON ME * A SINNER**

A BIBLICAL PRAYER

The *Jesus Prayer* is a Gospel prayer; it is a simple prayer; it is a profound prayer; it is a prayer for everyone. In the eighteenth chapter of St Luke's Gospel we find the parable of the proud and hypocritical Pharisee, multiplying words, extolling himself, and looking down upon the poor tax collector who is aware of his wrongdoing and unworthiness. The tax collector's prayer is simple and poor, but God hears it. It is: 'God be merciful to me, a sinner' (vv. 9–14).

Then in verses 35–43 we find the story of the healing of the blind man at Jericho, who calls repeatedly, persistently and savingly: 'Jesus, Son of David, have mercy on me!'

The Jesus Prayer is a combination of these two prayers, in the realization that we need forgiveness, healing and spiritual sight:

Lord Jesus Christ,
Son of God,
Have mercy on me,
a sinner.

I begin my day at 4.30 am with a few minutes of biblical praying, and then move into the *Jesus Prayer* which moves from the lips, to the mind, and is meant to descend to the heart. Sometimes the prayer time is taken up very powerfully by the Lord, and I feel a certain passivity in that I am 'prayed through', as if I am the Lord's flute through which he breathes his Holy Spirit, producing music, melody and adoration. Sometimes the time of prayer is difficult and my repetition of the name of Jesus is by faith, leading me to patience, stillness, waiting. And sometimes the prayer takes varying forms which I will explain in the next two chapters. But let me describe its basic and simple form.

REPETITION

Jesus warned against the repetition of empty phrases in prayer (Matthew 6:7), because there is a Pharisaism of the vain multiplication of words before others as a work of merit to gain favour with God. But Jesus also does honour to the repetition of persistent and dogged faith as with the blind man. And there is certainly a repetition of adoration as the angelic throng praise God unceasingly day and night (Isaiah 6:1–8; Revelation 4:6–11; 5:11–14). This is a glimpse of the universal and cosmic adoration of God the Father through the redeeming love of Christ the Son, inspired by the inbreathing of the Holy Spirit.

In the faithful repetition of the *Jesus Prayer* the believer is caught up into this unending worship, adoration and glory, and by being exposed to such light and fire, the structures of the believer's own being are transfigured by the divine glory. In the repetition there is rhythm, simplicity and continuity, as the body, mind and spirit are moved into the love and compassion of God. This is the very place where that amazing transfiguration occurs, spoken of by St Paul in 2 Corinthians 3:18:

> *And all of us, with unveiled faces, seeing the glory of the Lord as though reflected in a mirror, are being transformed into the same image from one degree of glory to another; for this comes from the Lord, the Spirit.*

LIPS, MIND AND HEART

There are three stages at which the prayer is experienced: with the lips (saying), with the mind (thinking), with the heart (feeling), though the dimension of the heart is infinite.

You keep the trysting time with God, and even though the mind is distracted or full of carnal desires, you say the prayer with the *lips*. Just repeat the name of Jesus and the Holy Spirit will ensure, as you continue, that the interior transformation will begin.

Then the prayer is taken over by the *mind*. This is not *cerebral* thinking; it is rather an intuitive awareness, a thoughtful attention and concentration on the prayer. If there is an invasion of the mind by 101 other distracting thoughts, don't fight them, simply return to the prayer . . . return to the prayer. Without strain or fear, simply return to the prayer. This stage may last for weeks, months, or even years, with irregular glimpses of the third stage. But the Lord is often gracious enough to draw us temporarily into an awareness of his gentle and fiery embrace, which is the experience of the third stage.

In this third stage the prayer descends to the *heart*. The lips are silent, the mind becomes quiet, and the prayer fills the cave of the heart, which is the centre of one's being.

There are many variations within this third stage, from the glimpses of the beginner which the Lord grants to create deeper hunger, to those who have dwelt within the name of Jesus for many years. There is a progressive resting in God, a flooding of the dark and dry inlets of the soul, and a refining of the gold in love's crucible so that the image of God may be reflected in its depths.

The great contemplatives recommend that the prayer be uttered silently according to the rhythm of the respiration or heartbeat, so that the whole body, mind and spirit are taken up into the prayer, and it becomes cosmic in its proportions. The human soul is a microcosm, containing in itself the image of the cosmos, and by means of the *Jesus Prayer* may feel itself to be a living and functioning part of the web of creation.

If you are drawn to this kind of meditative prayer, be assured that it is a prayer for simple believers, for those growing in grace, and for saintly men and women who long to love God more. Like the river in the forty-seventh chapter of Ezekiel, there are waters in which to paddle, to wade, to swim; and depths beyond the imagination, flowing from the throne of God. You can imagine the feelings of a young Greek or Russian novice receiving the prayer rope of 100 knots, preparing to wade and swim in the waters of God's love.

HOW TO DO IT

- Find a quiet place where you will not be disturbed;
- Sit or kneel on a prayer stool, relaxed, yet alert, with straight back;
- Relax each part of your body from the soles of your feet to the crown of your head;
- Note the rhythm of your breathing, and then let it become a little slower, a little deeper, finding your own relaxed level. Be gentle with yourself. No forcing, but surrendering to the presence and breathing of the Holy Spirit;
- After a period of relaxed breathing, begin gently to repeat the fourfold prayer:

Lord Jesus Christ,
Son of God,
have mercy on me,
a sinner.

As you go on you will find out how important are posture, relaxation, and loose clothing when using the prayer to the breath or heartbeat.

It is worth joining a group to establish the practice. In Glasgow we had a chaplaincy group meeting for the *Jesus Prayer* on alternate Fridays. The Fridays between were for our Amnesty International meeting. One fed the other.

Apart from my early morning use of the *Jesus Prayer*, I sometimes take my knotted rope and walk the prayer through the fields, when the context is so very different from my morning darkness. There are other variations which I will now go on to describe, but let me conclude this chapter with the words which I supply with each of the prayer stools I construct. They are from the Theophan the Recluse:

> *I will remind you of only one thing: one must descend with the mind into the heart, and there stand before the face of the Lord, ever present, all-seeing within you. The prayer takes a firm and steadfast hold, when a small fire begins to burn in the heart. Try not to quench this fire, and it will become established in such a way that the prayer repeats itself: and then you will have within you a small murmuring stream.*

12

A Healing Variation
on The Jesus Prayer

THE BASIC PRAYER

I have been using the *Jesus Prayer* in its basic form, as described
in the last chapter, for over twenty years, and it has become
the foundation of my contemplative life, for it most beautifully
unites the biblical cry for salvation with the increasing awareness of the divine presence in the depths of my heart. Have you
ever done the exercise of composing an epitaph for your grave-
stone which would encapsulate the meaning of your life? Well,
my chosen words would be simply these:

Lord Jesus Christ,
Son of God,
Have mercy on me,
a sinner.

Over the last two years or so, although the basic prayer retains
the foundational place it has always had, I have found a certain
variation in its use for a particular need. The need was for
physical healing during the third and fourth years of my exploration of the hermit life. I will not call it a development or
evolution of the prayer, but rather a variation, because there

will be some users of the prayer who will not want its basic simplicity to be compromised in any way, for its simplicity is the primary thing for them.

Certainly, the basic words, with nothing added, but repeated and leading to interior contemplation is just what is needed for the Christian who is being led by God into a deeper interior life, or who is in desperate need and cannot manage verbose or sophisticated prayers or methods which are cerebral instead of intuitive and simple.

But my experience of a healing variation of the prayer fitted my need, and it may speak to some who have a particular physical or mental dis-ease (in both senses) which needs to be exposed to the healing love of God. This may be the case for a specific sickness, stress or anxiety, or as an occasional variation in which the prayer is used for others in intercession for the healing of the world's ills. It is because I have passed on this healing variation to others in particular need that I include it here, for they have indicated its positive value for healing at various levels.

THE HEALING VARIATION

Because of a specific need for healing, and realizing my need to open my body, mind and spirit to the saving and healing power of God, I found myself praying the *Jesus Prayer* in a new way. Let me describe it first, and then go on to expound its particular relevance and meaning: The variation is four-fold:

1 *Lord Jesus Christ/Son of God,*
   Let your healing flow down/upon me;
2 *Lord Jesus Christ/Son of God,*
   Let your healing spring up/within me;
3 *Lord Jesus Christ/Son of God,*
   Let your healing love/enfold me;
4 *Lord Jesus Christ/Son of God,*
   Let your healing power/flow through me.

ATTITUDE AND MEANING

The *Jesus Prayer* itself, though in a petitionary form, directs the believer to contemplative prayer. This variation is not a cajoling or begging prayer to persuade a reluctant God to grant a desperate petition. Rather, it is a prayer to bring the believer into an attitude of expectant receptivity – that place where the generous saving and healing power of God may flow into and through the whole person. Its aim is to concentrate the heart and mind of the Christian upon the divine Love which is the fountain from which all forgiveness and healing flow.

If sin is forgiven, the heart set upon God, and the whole being open and waiting, then those barriers which keep God's merciful grace at bay will be breached and the floodgates will be opened, admitting the healing river of love into the dry places of the soul.

Now let us look at the meaning of these prayers. At first I began with the *Jesus Prayer* itself, then when I felt prepared and ready, I repeated each of the above prayers three times, and then returned to the basic *Jesus Prayer*, and silence. As soon as you get the feel of the prayers and they are rooted firmly in your mind and heart, then they become easy and natural to pray in the context of the basic *Jesus Prayer*. Simply, that is all that is involved.

1 The first prayer is: '*let your healing flow down upon me*'. This is directed to Christ as the *Pantocrator* – Mighty One, the transcendent Christ who gazes into the believer's heart from the dome of an Orthodox church or icon. You may also think of the ever deepening river of God flowing from God's heart, bringing life and fertility wherever it goes. My desire is that this transcendent blessing, this healing river, may flow over and into me, bringing physical healing, forgiveness and peace.

2 The second prayer is: '*let your healing spring up within me*'. Here is an acknowledgment that God's Holy Spirit dwells within me and that my body is a temple of the Spirit, awaiting the rising spring of healing and restorative powers that already reside within. This prayer is directed towards the immanent Christ – the interior, indwelling mystery of Christ within, the hope of glory (Colossians 1:27). The image is a quiet, bubbling spring of healing water, a gentle, murmuring stream which, when the rubble is cleared away from its source, will spring up into every crevice of my being. It reminds me of Jesus' description of the Spirit-filled Christian: 'Out of the believer's heart shall flow rivers of living water.' (John 7:38).

3 The third prayer is: '*let your healing love enfold me*'. If Christ is transcendent *above* me, and immanent *within* me, he also completely surrounds me, enfolding, caressing, holding us within himself, like a protected child is enfolded within the loving embrace of its mother. This is not a regress to the embracing womb in fear of the wicked world, but rather a directed retreat into the divine Love, so that sustained and

111

restored, I may return to the world as a witness to God's compassionate embrace.

4 The fourth prayer is: '*let your healing power flow through me*'. This is the affirmation that God's healing power does not stagnate in an interior lake, with no outlet. Love always flows, and we are the channels of its communication. If I experience the forgiveness, the healing, the peace of God, then I shall become a source of such blessings to other lives. The indwelling Spirit will flow through me and affect those around me, either physically or via my prayers and compassion.

RETURN TO THE JESUS PRAYER

This fourfold variation emerges from, and returns to, the *Jesus Prayer*. The *Jesus Prayer* is basic, and if we are in desperate straits, physically or spiritually, there may be a breakdown of all the thought processes and images involved in this variation. Then we must simply cast ourselves unreservedly upon the merciful love of God and cry out: '*Lord Jesus Christ, Son of God, have mercy on me, a sinner*'. God knows my mortal need and I do not have to present richly ornamented liturgical prayers in such a situation, but simply gasp, like Peter sinking in the water: 'Lord, save me!'

We must also understand that the *Jesus Prayer* itself is simply part of the whole Church's prayer of worship and adoration. It is part of humankind's yearning and response to the Spirit of God, part of the deep river of prayer which flows from the divine fecundity of grace, through the cosmic order, and returns to the bosom of the Godhead who is our ultimate home.

13

An Intercessory Variation on The Jesus Prayer

TRUE PRAYER HAS COSMIC IMPLICATIONS

In the two previous chapters I have spoken of prayer as the river of God which flows from the heart of God, through the created order, and back to the bosom of the Godhead. Now I want to suggest that this river is an underground river, flowing through the whole of humanity, expressing itself in the profoundest joys and sorrows in the heights and depths of our humanity. We are coming to see more clearly that the universe is an interrelated web of pulsating life, and that what happens in one corner of the cosmos has universal implications for the whole, and that makes it vitally important that our lives are given to wholesome good and not to disintegrating evil, for our lives will cause ripples of good or evil throughout the universe.

I think of this river, then, as the underground river of compassion, and that by the gift of prayer we may become consciously united with the wholeness of things, and through our praying we can offer ourselves, our vital strength, our very souls as an offering of love and healing in order that the world may come at last to reconciliation and healing. I believe this is what St Paul is referring to in that mysterious statement he makes in Colossians 1:24: 'I am now rejoicing in my sufferings for your sake, and in my flesh I am completing what is lacking in Christ's afflictions for the sake of his body, that is, the church.' How can *anything* be added to the completed and finished work of Christ which he wrought for our salvation? Yet if we think of this statement of St Paul, and of the *stigmata* of St Francis, in which he entered in body and spirit to share the suffering and death of Christ, then we may see that we are invited, even called, into the fellowship of his sufferings, for the world's healing.

There are a number of ways in which this may be done. The simplest act of self-sacrificial love and the offering of your life in martyrdom both share in its glory. But it is here, in the practice of the *Jesus Prayer*, that you may really experience that pulsating flow of the underground river of compassion. True prayer is loving communion with God, and personal prayer is taken up into the corporate nature of the communion of saints and into the eternal prayer that Christ offers continually to the Father.

Between the simplest infant prayers of petition and the highest level of contemplative union with God there is the whole area of intercession – prayer for others. For us this is sometimes the most difficult area, for God knows their needs more than we do, loves them more than we do, and what can we say that will add to what is already in his heart for them? The best way in for me is the understanding that my prayers are a response to the Holy Spirit within, the blending of my loving concern for others within the greater divine Love that shines with compassion in the dark places of the earth. It is, in fact, God within praying to the God above – love answering love for the accomplishing of his will through me. I become an instrument of God's compassion, the flute through which the breath of God blows, bringing about the ultimate healing harmony which is the will of God being done on earth as it is in heaven.

Therefore, it does not matter whether my intercessions are verbal, laying before God all the areas of conflict, hopes and fears of humankind, or simply the silent holding up of the world before him in faith. But a form of words can sometimes be helpful to me, or to a group who engage in intercessory prayer for individuals or nations.

THE JESUS PRAYER FOR INTERCESSION

The form of the *Jesus Prayer* is already petitionary. In order to keep its form and use it as intercession, I sometimes put myself in the place of my suffering friend, that needy family, those victimized prisoners or that war-torn nation and pray the same words, but now as if from their mouths and hearts:

Lord Jesus Christ,
Son of God,
Have mercy on me,
a sinner.

When I began to use the *Jesus Prayer* for healing, I explained in the last chapter, how I used the fourfold variation in order to enter more deeply into the healing grace of God by looking to the transcendent Christ to pour his healing *upon* me, to the indwelling Christ to allow his healing to spring up *within* me, to the surrounding Christ to let his healing *enfold* me, and to the communing Christ to release his healing power *through* me.

As I was already using the basic *Jesus Prayer* for intercession, so now I began to use the healing variation, simply changing the *me* into *us*, or *them*, as appropriate. I began, as usual, with the basic prayer, then held those for whom I was praying, within the love of God, repeating three times with each form:

1 *Lord Jesus Christ/Son of God,*
  Let your healing flow down/upon us (them);
2 *Lord Jesus Christ/Son of God,*
  Let your healing spring up/within us (them);
3 *Lord Jesus Christ/Son of God,*
  Let your healing love/enfold us (them);
4 *Lord Jesus Christ/Son of God,*
  Let your healing power/flow through us (them).

then I return to the basic *Jesus Prayer*. This can be repeated as often as needed or for different people and situations, beginning and ending with the basic prayer.

The positive value of this way of praying in intercession is that I can hold up the individual or situation before God for *healing*; and that can mean forgiveness of sins, healing of the body or mind, or alleviation of suffering and reconciliation in a situation of cruelty, war or injustice. Also the prayer is addressed to God *above*, to God *within*, to God *around*, and to the God who is present in and through all things.

Indeed, the more I use this form of prayer and the more I reflect upon it, the more it yields a deeper meaning, enriching and enhancing my own life of concern and intercession. This, in turn, leads to sharing and action for the greater common good.

But don't be too ambitious. Do not attempt this variation until you are grounded in the use of the basic *Jesus Prayer*. Otherwise it will be confusing, and you will land yourself in the error of using your brain to pray; this kind of praying must be natural, easy and flowing, and if you are constantly groping for words it is counterproductive.

BEGINNING AND ENDING IN GOD

As we have seen, prayer has cosmic implications, and if we are able to take this larger and universal view of prayer, then we shall understand that however weak and struggling are our prayers of intercession, and however helpless we may feel in the face of the world's suffering, cruelty and injustice, we shall feel that we are making some small contribution to its healing in its wider sense. We shall also realize that we are caught up into the worldwide network of prayer that sustains us as we weave our small patch in the cosmic pattern which is part of God's redemptive process.

As the *Jesus Prayer* makes clear, the cross is at the heart of the world's redemption, for it is directed towards Christ as Redeemer, the crucified and risen Son of God. The redeeming cross is not only planted at the centre of the world's history, but its light shines back to the foundation of the world, and on into eternity. And if the redeeming work of Christ is a cosmic work, then the nature of prayer is also cosmic, beginning and ending in the divine Love.

As a young Christian I used to think of the head of the cross emerging from the Father's heart, the foot of the cross planted into the world's sin and suffering, and the two arms of the cross outstretched in compassion and invitation in the words of Jesus: 'Come to Me . . .' (Matthew 11:28).

This intercessory variation on the *Jesus Prayer* may give you some insight into the nature of intercessory prayer, and may even start you off on a possible way of praying for the world, which previously had been problematic. Certainly, prayers of intercession become a mingling of petition, thanksgiving and adoration – the place where heaven and earth join in the life of the praying Christian. The personal and the corporate blend in the disciplined offering of compassionate prayer – remember that underground river of love – and such praying is heard and answered in the mystery of God.

The Monastery Track

14

Making a Pilgrimage

HUMAN PILGRIMAGE

We all go on pilgrimage. It is part of our human yearning to
associate places with people we love, with experiences which are
precious, with events which are holy, and such places may be
imbued with sanctity renewing our dedication, stimulating our
devotion and imparting a sense of healing, holiness and peace.

Each year my one pilgrimage from my hut-enclosure is to
my home town, Swansea, for there are numerous places in and
around that location which are sacred to my childhood, and
wandering around the coastline and peninsula evokes mem-
ories of joys, sorrows and yearnings which continue to give
direction to my life. Last year my sister and I made our annual
pilgrimage to the cemetery where mother and father lie, and
after tidying and arranging flowers before the simple oak cross,
we held hands together and prayed, with some tears. It was a
pilgrimage.

Such a pilgrimage to the graveside of a loved one, with
its reminder of our mortality, is a reflection of our life's
pilgrimage from cradle to grave. All of us are on this journey,
and all our pretensions, ambitions, wealth and power come to
an end at this place.

A HOLY PLACE

The persistence of a sense of pilgrimage is remarkable. I have
Catholic friends who regularly go on pilgrimage to Lourdes
and other holy places as part of their spirituality. And I have
other Welsh Nonconformist friends who would not go near
Lourdes, but would make a pilgrimage, say prayers and sing
hymns at the graves of William Williams, Pantycelyn, or Ann
Griffiths, those saintly hymn writers.

There are the classic holy places for the Christian, like
the Holy Land itself, followed by Rome, Assisi, Canterbury,
Santiago da Compostella, or the Celtic holy places of Britain
such as the islands of Lindisfarne, Iona or Bardsey. Jerusalem is
the supreme holy place, loved not only by Christians but also
by Jews and Muslims.

While the faithful people of every tradition go on their
pilgrimages with devotion and intense fervour, the saintly ones
know that unless God is to be found within their own experience, such pilgrimage is useless. The mystic Kabir puts it
succinctly:

> I laugh when I hear that the fish
> in the water is thirsty:
> You wander restlessly from forest to forest,
> while the reality is within your dwelling.
> The truth is here! Go where you will,
> to Benares or to Mathura,
> Until you have found God in your own soul
> the whole world will seem meaningless to you.

and St Augustine makes a similar point:

> *People go abroad to wonder at the height of mountains, at the huge waves of the sea, at the long courses of the rivers, at the vast compasses of the ocean, at the circular motion of the stars, and they pass themselves by without wondering.*

Yet it is true that a place may be hallowed by presence, by miracle, by a mighty revelation, and it may become a site of holiness, of renewal, of healing or life-giving power. The waters of Lourdes, of Walsingham, of St Non's well at St David's — here baptism may take place, holy water may be splashed and sprinkled. It was doubtless thought superstitious that the paralysed man in John 5:1–9 waited for the angelic troubling of the waters for his healing. But as he waited, Jesus came to him and fulfilled his heart's desire.

If you make an effort to get to a holy place of pilgrimage, with an open and expectant heart you will find great joy in the fellowship of your fellow pilgrims around a place sanctified by prayer and the communion of saints. It was with tremendous anticipation that I heard the following words at the hermit symposium at St David's in 1975, beginning a week of silence, prayer and fellowship:

> *I want to begin with a very simple affirmation. I believe that the question we have come to study here together during these days is one of vital importance not only for the whole Church, but for all mankind. We have come purposely to a place which seems marginal, and we shall be talking about a way of life which, in our time at least, seems particularly marginal. Yet, as I shall hope*

to suggest, the place of the solitary is only in appearance at the edge; in reality he is the one who stands at the very heart of things.

The place where we are meeting, St David's, itself may help us to understand a little more of this paradox. Geographically today it is remote and inaccessible, an eminently marginal place. In another age when, however difficult and dangerous sea travel was, it was at least less perilous than travel by land, its position was altogether different. It was one of the focal places of Celtic Christendom, a centre both of cenobitic and eremitic monasticism. *

A HOLY PERSON

Bill, a Baptist minister friend, loves leading pilgrimages to the Holy Land, and he has a deep devotion to the Jewish people. He (as a Baptist!) lights candles for me at holy sites, and follows the *Via Dolorosa* where Jesus carried his cross to Calvary.

I remember that when we were about eighteen, he came on the pillion seat of my motor cycle and we made a 'pilgrimage' to Earl's Court to share in the Billy Graham Evangelistic Rally and heard the singer Beverley Shea sing a song of pilgrimage to the Holy Land, concluding with the lines:

I walked today where Jesus walked,
And felt him close to me.

Christians of all denominations will make pilgrimage to the Holy Land because our Saviour was born in a cave in

* A. M. Allchin (ed.), *Solitude and Communion*, (op. cit.) p.1.

Bethlehem, walked the hills of Galilee, climbed Tabor, Hermon, the Mount of Olives, healed the sick in Capernaum, did miracles at Bethany, agonized in Gethsemane and died on Calvary. Many Christians will also take the thorny road of pilgrimage wherever the radiance of sanctity has shone through the person and works of God's saints. They will travel to the catacombs or the holy sites of martyrdom, or to the gravesides of saints like Seraphim who encouraged his penitents to visit his grave after his death to talk with him simply, trustingly as of old, within the communion of saints.

Even if you cannot make the pilgrimage geographically, you can do it in spirit. Indeed, the imagination is called into play in reading the Gospels and praying them through meditatively. James Montgomery's hymn encourages the believer to follow Christ through the last hours of his life to the moment of his triumphant cry:

> Go to dark Gethsemane
>   You who feel the Tempter's power;
> Your Redeemer's conflict see,
>   Watch with him one bitter hour:
> Turn not from his griefs away,
> Learn of Jesus Christ to pray.

I am constantly humbled when people make Glasshampton a place of pilgrimage. Father William who, from 1918 to 1936 occupied Glasshampton and converted it from stables to a monastery, is buried in the garth,* and many people have

---

* See Geoffrey Curtis CR, *William of Glasshampton*, (SCM Press, 1978).

found salvation, renewal, healing and guidance here, as a place of pilgrimage.

I think of John who cycled from the other side of Birmingham with a light-weight trailer behind his bike, and Ronald whose sense of pilgrimage is clear:

> As a practical step, I left home the day before I was due to arrive at Glasshampton, and stayed the night in Worcester without booking a room in advance. That meant that I was more than usually detached from the normal routine by which I know each day where I shall be sleeping that night. I travelled by public transport — I have no car — and I packed the minimum, and used a rucksack instead of a suitcase so that I could walk from Worcester.

Stephen hitched from London, arriving at Shrawley, and he sets the scene to begin his week of silence in the monastery hut:

> I turned my back to the village and walked up the long track to the monastery, I walked slowly, taking in the trees and ploughed fields. It's important not to rush this part of the withdrawal, to allow the rolling fields to reflect my thoughts and feelings, to withdrawing to rather than from. I am excited and apprehensive, this is my first completely solitary hut retreat. The hut is really a hut. There is a bed, a chair, a table, a gas cooker, and an icon — Rublev's Trinity. The only lighting is by candle.

Last evening Robin and I knelt before the *Vladimir* icon in my hut chapel at the end of his pilgrimage retreat, and he was close to tears as he realized that the Lord had delivered him from a wrong direction in his pilgrimage, and set his feet back on firm ground. These few illustrate the increasing number of pilgrims wending their way to the divine Love.

MAKING YOUR OWN PILGRIMAGE

There are doubtless places of pilgrimage within reach of your area that you could undertake as an individual or with a group from your church or prayer group. Walking pilgrimages are often organized, sleeping in church halls along the way — for instance on a Canterbury pilgrimage to the spot in the cathedral where Thomas à Becket was martyred in 1170. If you have a love for the Celtic tradition there are walking pilgrimages to St David's patron's shrine, or to Bardsey Island where there is the blessed risk of being cut off — en-isled with God for extra time! Those who make a pilgrimage to Iona once hear that pilgrims always return to make it three times. I've made that wonderful journey twice.

Let me illustrate by telling you of one of my favourite pilgrimage places. It is the church, cell and holy well of St Issui at Patricio in the Black Mountains, just below Offa's Dyke in Wales — just a few miles from Llantony Abbey. If you look at your map, find the A465 between Hereford and Abergavenny. You will find marked the village of Llanfihangel Crucorney. From there the road ascends and narrows until you reach the high place of Patricio with an overwhelming and panoramic view of grandeur and serenity.

If you approach from the A40 Brecon to Abergavenny road, take the turn to Crickhowell and Llanbedr which will bring you to Patricio. Geographical directions sound mundane and pedestrian, but if you are fit enough to do the last few miles by foot, or even if you have to take your vehicle up to the holy well which lies in the dingle a few hundred yards below the church, you will soon be caught up to heaven.

The church at Patricio is simple, beautiful and with a silence which is palpable. The lovely medieval rood screen remains because the iconoclastic reformers missed the church in the mountains. The foundation began way back about the seventh century when Issui, a hermit, set up his wattle or wooden cell in the dingle, through which runs Nant Mair (St Mary's stream). He sanctified the well by baptising pilgrims and filling the whole place with prayer. The approach to the well is marked by a pilgrim stone bearing the Maltese cross, and in the spring enclosure there are small niches which once held the figures of saints.

The desert tradition carries stories of attacks upon hermits, and here it was no different, for Issui was murdered by an ungrateful traveller, but because of his saintly reputation the well became a place of pilgrimage and evidenced healing qualities. In the early eleventh century a continental pilgrim was so grateful for the healing of his leprosy at the well that he donated the gold to build a church on the hill above the well, dedicated to St Issui. This is now the chapel-cell which has been refurbished and was rededicated and opened for prayer by the Bishop in 1991. The present main church was built on to the eastern aspect of this chapel-cell.

I've often made a pilgrimage to this holy place with its stone seat and preaching cross outside the church, and its wide, expansive view of the lower Grwyney Fawr with the Usk in the far distance, and I've often coveted the hermit cell for myself!

During my three years at Tymawr I conducted no services and accepted no engagements. The exception was the young peoples' week when I led some teaching meditations, at the end of which we made a pilgrimage from Tymawr to Patricio with some of the sisters. When we reached the holy well after the long ascent, we gathered round, while Fr Christopher, the parish priest, and I shared the story of St Issui, and each pilgrim was marked with the sign of the cross from the well.

Then, singing 'Guide me O Thou great Redeemer', we puffed up the steep hill in procession, through the lich-gate, and were filled with wonder as we were exposed to the wide spaces and high sky on a clear and brilliant day. We entered into the silence of the church, circling the altar for the celebration of the Eucharist. This was a holy place and we were participating in the residual holiness and contributing to it in our worship and love of God.

After the Eucharist we sat on the stone seat around the preaching cross and shared our lunch together, mingled with the friendship and joy of one another in that high place of pilgrimage. It was quite different to my previous solitary and twosome pilgrimages, but containing its own enthusiasm and joy.

I have recently had an invitation from Fr Christopher inviting me to lead a healing service at the well, a pilgrimage walk to the church with evensong and homily. It was with sadness that I had to decline the invitation, but I am glad to know that Patricio continues as a place of prayer, healing and pilgrimage under the care of a priest whose love and joy was manifest in our sharing together.

God does not dwell in holy places made with hands, but in the hearts of his faithful people, for they are the temple of God.

Holy places are where the people of God gather for prayer and worship, and pilgrimage is not an ascetic and arduous journey of merit to find a faraway, transcendent God who separates himself from his creation. It is a journey, a celebration, a communion of love and faith in the God who has himself come to us in Christ.

If these things are true in our experience, then we can value aright the places where God has especially manifested his presence in days gone by, or which have been irradiated by the outshining of his holiness in his saints, and have been sanctified by miracle and prayer. T. S. Eliot captures the sense of a holy place in *Little Gidding*, the last section of his *Four Quartets*:

> *If you came this way,*
> *Taking any route, starting from anywhere,*
> *At any time or at any season,*
> *it would always be the same: you would have to put off*
> *sense and notion. You are not here to verify,*
> *Instruct yourself, or inform curiosity*
> *Or carry report. You are here to kneel*
> *Where prayer has been valid. And prayer is more*
> *Than an order of words, the conscious occupation*
> *Of the praying mind, or the sound of the voice praying.*

Be encouraged then to make such a pilgrimage, light a candle of prayer at such a place in intercession for a needy brother or sister, and bring back some water from the holy well. The holy places of the Bible will become more precious in your meditations, and it will be a further experience of grace on your greater pilgrimage to God.

15

A Walking Meditation

SIMPLY WALKING

There is no lofty aim or purpose in this meditation. It is not a 'meditation upon something' or done in order to attain anything, to pursue anything, to accomplish anything – it is simply walking. It may be thought of as an exercise in awareness, but this is said in order that you should do the walking aware of what you are doing in that present moment – mindfully.

In my enclosure I have marked out a straight path, from the Celtic cross which stands outside my chapel hut to a small apple tree which holds an icon of the risen Christ. It measures thirty-three easy steps for the years of Jesus' life, and this helps me to walk in his steps (1 Peter 2:21) and enables me to walk mindfully without counting.

I stand still and quiet at the cross, hands joined lightly in front, facing the icon. I begin walking slowly, measuredly, eyes a few paces in front, placing one foot before another, composedly, with no hurry, no strain, but easily, simply walking. When I reach the icon, I stand still for a few breaths, turn, and walk back to the cross. I continue walking, pausing, turning, walking, for fifteen to twenty minutes, stand still in thankfulness. And that's it!

WHAT IS HAPPENING?

What's happening? Well nothing need happen — I simply walk. But of course, because I am who I am, all sorts of things do happen, and different things on different days. But I don't do the walk in order to *make* things happen, to manipulate the walk or myself. I have no aims or ambitions in the walk — it is simply walking. In this way I do not become disappointed if I am neither elated or inspired, or when it does not yield what it did the last time.

But let me share with you the walking meditation which I did this morning, though this is not a repetition of what happened last time or what will happen next time. Neither do I want you to press your walking meditation into a similar mould to mine. You are you, and what happens, or does not happen, to you is yours and no one else's. You may become ecstatic; you may become melancholy and disappointed; you may reach neither heights nor depths, but simply walk mindfully — and perhaps that is how it is meant to be.

WALKING THIS MORNING

I stood still, gathering my concentration, breathing slowly, relaxing my whole body, and began to walk. I set one foot before another, feeling my feet within my shoes, the texture of the earth beneath my feet, aware of my balance, the movement of my limbs, the easy pace, the ground covered, and the simple joy of walking.

As I walked, paused, turned, walked . . . I became more

aware of the October morning, the slight breeze, the autumn sun, the changing, falling leaves, the clear day, the fields around, the noise of partridges and crows, the cows in the adjoining field.

Still walking . . . not encouraging or discouraging thoughts, the reality of the season pressed upon me. The dying of the year, the trees and shrubs around my enclosure losing their foliage, the exposed skeleton of bare branches – all the lovely melancholy of late October.

As I walk this linear path I am aware of my own dying, finitude, mortality. My leaves are falling, seasons slip away, I am a pilgrim setting one foot before another on my own mortal journey. One foot before another, one step, another step, keep on walking, mindfully, gently, thankfully. I am tempted to develop my thinking, to 'make a meditation', to construct a homily. But I let it go, establish my concentrated awareness again – and keep on walking . . . walking . . . walking. Then I reach the cross once more and stop. I take some deep breaths, feel a quiet sense of gratitude, and return to my hut.

NO BIG DEAL

Does this merit a place in a book on spirituality? There is hardly a mention or thought of God, no prayers, no invocation, resolution or transfiguration. Even a child could do it. But yes, that is the point; that there is no point, save that I walk for walking's sake. And though I do not plan a purpose or achieve a particular aim, there is today an overflow of gentle tranquillity.

If there were not, it would not worry me, for I do not hope to recapture the past, or seek guidance for the future. It is simply an exercise in awareness, a walking in mindfulness — and I commend it to you.

16

Finding a Soul Friend

WHAT IS A SOUL FRIEND?

Rather than offer a traditional definition, I've just done a brainstorming enquiry into what I need in a soul friend, and I've come up with the following:

You are my soul friend if:

- *as a father or mother you love and care for me in my spiritual childhood:*
- *as a brother or sister you open yourself to me as I to you in complete trust, with no holds barred, in mutual help, laughter and tears;*
- *as a spiritual physician you diagnose and prescribe for my soul's good;*
- *as a fellow-pilgrim you take my hand, negotiating the obstacles, perplexities and ecstasies of our shared journey;*
- *as a wounded healer you listen to me with understanding and counsel me with compassion when I expose my wounds to your gaze;*
- *as a mature and informed guide you apply the counsel of the prayer-tradition to my thinking mind and my yearning heart;*
- *as a confessor and believer-priest you mediate God's loving forgiveness and constant direction on the way of holiness and humanity.*

There are a number of personalized metaphors there, all to do with spiritual direction, but the basis is friendship, mutual love and compassionate fraternal relationship. It's a tall order as you'll appreciate, and perhaps the archangel Gabriel would be hard put to in applying for the job! But I know that with various people I have been on the receiving end of such compassionate care, and have been able, under God, to embrace brothers and sisters in such spiritual friendship. The cost is high both in the care I have received and in the spiritual energy given, and this is indicated in the story of the woman with chronic haemorrhage when she *felt* healing power flow into her, and Jesus *felt* healing power flowing from him; the Greek word is *dunamis* (Mark 5:30), and dynamic power it certainly was.

THE WHOLE OF LIFE

Although I like the term *soul friend* (spiritual director is also useful), it is not simply a matter of *soul* guidance, as if the spiritual dimension is to be compartmentalized. The word is inclusive, and means that the whole of one's life is open to God for orientation into health, love and holiness. God is concerned with my physical wellbeing, my bodily health, my sexual maturity, my mental liveliness and my spiritual awareness and wholeness. There may be profound spiritual reasons why I am obsessed with guilt, frenetically active and unreasonably angry, and there may be physical reasons why I am frequently depressed or sexually frustrated.

The reason why so many people are paying expensive fees to

psychiatrists (who have their place) is because they do not open themselves to a compassionate soul friend in confession and honesty. There is immense joy in sharing our 'highs' as well as confessing our 'lows', and I am persuaded that the encouragement found in James 5:16 is not confined to sacramental confession, but is a mark of a spiritually healthy believer and congregation: 'Confess your sins to one another, and pray for one another, so that you may be healed'.

MATURITY A NECESSITY

I do not mean simply that we should all be soul friends to everybody, all of the time. We would be exhausted, and it would be inappropriate. There should be a mutuality and sharing among all God's people, of course, but there is a special gift and discernment needed in spiritual direction. The word 'maturity' is an appropriate one because it has to do with an all-rounded person. Not necessarily a professional theologian or listening therapist, but one who has reached a personal maturity and wisdom through the positive and negative experiences of life, with a basic acquaintance with the theological foundation of our Faith and an understanding of traditional and contemporary spirituality.

When an evangelical Christian enters into charismatic blessing, then sooner or later there will be darkness, perplexity and doubts. Therefore a soul friend who has a Catholic understanding of the 'dark night' will be needed. And when a traditional Catholic who has been faithful to church duties and a disciplined moral life feels the weight and burden of a lifeless churchianity, then a soul friend is needed; one who can lead the arid spirit into the fertile spirituality of a personal assurance in Christ and an experience of the indwelling of the Holy Spirit.

There is hidden treasure in the Catholic and evangelical traditions, there are pitfalls, as well as blessings, in the charismatic and liberal traditions, and the soul friend who has knowledge and experience of breadth and depth in the Church of God is all too rare. That is why I am constantly having requests to find a spiritual director for the many Christians who realize their need of clear direction in their lives of prayer and discipleship.

It is easy to blame the scarcity on the Church, though it is sad constantly to find non-Christians and Christians who experience the Church as an obstacle to Christ instead of a witness to the saving and reconciling Gospel. Certainly, priests and pastors should be mature in faith, trained in spirituality, ascetic in discipline and full of the Holy Spirit — and some of them are. But there are at least two problems here. One is that the demands made upon them are excessive as they are expected to function spiritually, socially and organizationally with increasing bureaucracy. And the second is that there are too few of them to give personal, in-depth ministry to the congregations under their care. As to the first problem, I believe that the individual priest must resist excessive expectations, and say 'no' to most committee meetings, laying down disciplined lines of priority in order to give attention to what Michael Ramsey wrote about in *The Charismatic Christ*:

Amid the spiritual hunger of our times, when many whose souls are starved by activism are seeking guidance in the contempla-

tion of God, a terrible judgement rests upon the priest who is unable to give help or guidance because he has ceased to be a man of prayer himself.

Those words were written over twenty years ago. Since then many men and women in professional ministry have acknowledged their gifts, and disciplined themselves in training for spiritual direction, but the second problem remains. There are too few, not least because the ordinary Christian has woken up to the spiritual path, and the whole dimension of Spirituality is buzzing with seekers, so that mature and trained soul friends are at a premium.

I believe that the spiritual life with all its implications cannot be left to professionals, many of whom are directionless themselves. Within the body of Christ there are men and women God is calling to a mature spirituality for themselves, opening out to a ministry of soul friendship for others.

My writing is aimed at such people. Of course it encourages me when fellow clergy appreciate what I have to teach and share, but when I find lay Christians combining my teaching with their own biblical insights and natural gifts in ministering to others, it gives me immense joy. The number is increasing, and to illustrate I think of Mark, who is a furniture designer and maker. After having spent some years in a disciplined path of study and contemplative prayer, he found that people were coming to his workshop for help and guidance, and he began to share what he himself was learning.

He described to me a recent prayer workshop which he led in a local retreat house. Each participant was given a 30" length of timber as they arrived. The first session began with teaching on 'The Holy Spirit and Creativity'. The second session was given over to the cutting, sanding, hingeing, polishing and finishing of individual prayer stools. The last session consisted of a guided meditation on some aspect of the life of prayer, using the meditation stools made during the day.

Mark began this specific part of his spiritual journey with me some nine years ago; he has since become a husband and a father, opening every part of his life to the Spirit's guidance as he has sensed the Lord's direction for him. His devotional life has kept up with his spiritual reading, and it is with great mutual profit that our letters flow between the annual visits to Glasshampton. Recently he wrote a paper, at my request, on 'Creativity and the Prayerful Presence of God', which makes clear the objectivity and reality of his discipleship and maturity.

I sometimes think it would be exciting for me and the reader if I were to chart out the stories of twelve such men and women who are in touch with me in spiritual friendship, so that the reader can see that they are ordinary Christians with an extraordinary sense of God's call and leading. They are all examples of Paul's counsel to his son and soul friend, Timothy:

You then, my child, be strong in the grace that is in Christ Jesus; and what you have heard from me through many witnesses entrust to faithful people who will be able to teach others as well.

(2 Timothy 2:1, 2).

FINDING A SOUL FRIEND

This brings us to the question of how to find a soul friend. Please don't add to those who write and ask me to recommend one. At the beginning of my hermit life I explained to the penitents (old-fashioned but good word) who came to me that I could no longer continue with them as a regular soul friend. I recommended them to others who would care for them, though they could come to me in a crisis or once only, which is my condition for seeing anyone now. But from among them I have seen the multiplication of soul friends on the Paul and Timothy principle. The main thrust of my teaching now is by prayer and writing, with the occasional meeting of a limited number. But I am feeling increasingly confident in the maturity, ability and effectiveness of these people. If any of them start asking questions about ordination I usually suggest they do not go in that direction unless they can't help it! There are too many of the wrong people in professional, salaried ministry, and let me add that I have a high view of priesthood in the Church of God, holding my vocation very dearly. But what we need today is an increasing group of men and women who are exercising their gifts of ministry – healing, counselling, group leadership, retreat conducting, and much more – all springing from soul friend relationships.

I must emphasize that this must not take place independently of the liturgical and sacramental life of the Church. It must supplement, not detract from, the Church's corporate life. Otherwise we adopt a sect mentality and soon fall into spiritual élitism and exclusivism, which shuts down on our precious humanity.

In his valuable book *Soul Friend*, Kenneth Leech writes of the sustaining maturity which is experienced and communicated by the true soul friend, using the biblical image of the shepherd:

> The Shepherd is one who feeds and nourishes the flock, makes the weak strong, seeks the lost, cares for the sick, and bandages the wounded (Ezek. 34.3–4; 15–16). This Shepherd image recurs frequently in the history of the cure of souls. In Ezekiel, the Shepherd is concerned not only with healing (34.16) but also with the achievement of harmony and of shalom, peace (34.24). And in the New Testament, there is a bringing together of the themes of the wounded healer, the slain lamb, the stricken shepherd, and the guide who nourishes the flock.

AN EMERGING VOCATION

What I am envisaging is the emergence of a vocation among lay folk to the task and privilege of soul friendship. This is already happening, for there are men and women of all the main line Christian churches, who are increasingly aware of who they are, of what the soul friendship tradition consists, and who have the communicative ability and love of their brothers and sisters to give themselves as channels of the Holy Spirit within the sustaining network of the Church of God. They are not ordained, professional or hierarchic, though a form of recognition and laying-on-of-hands would be appropriate. This would be a wider recognition of their validity and authority for such a task, making them responsible to the wider network, and would weed out the many people who would 'covet' any counselling role in order to shore up their own fragile egos. Beware of self-appointed prophets or counsellors!

Already it is easier to find a soul friend than it was twenty years ago when only priests, pastors and religious were thought to be the real thing. Because a person is ordained, or a religious, that does not automatically mean that they are gifted for soul friendship, though many will continue to come from those categories. Increasingly the network of soul friends and spiritual directors will spread within the Church, and training by experience will supplement the mind and heart knowledge of the great tradition.

To know oneself is the basic requirement, and knowing oneself in the path of following Christ imparts also the knowledge of others. There are many paths and methods, disciplines and techniques within the way of Christ, and the appropriate pattern for a particular pilgrim will be part of the discernment of a true soul friend or spiritual director.

As well as possessing personal charismatic gifts for this ministry, you will also need the training that gives objectivity and shape to such a ministry, and that is increasingly available through study and sharing in the diverse spiritualities across the denominational board today.

So we are left with two important matters at the end of this chapter. The first is that part of the answer to the question of finding a soul friend for yourself is to look for a fellow Christian, not necessarily a priest, and not particularly of your own communion. If you feel the need of clear direction then look up to God in faith and look around within the fellowship of believers. A number of my friends have soul friends of other denominations, and this imparts sparkle, variety, humility and ecumenical unity to their spiritual quest.

The second matter is that you may be led, in putting yourself under the discipline of spiritual direction, to realize an emerging vocation in your own life — to become a soul friend to another, to a group, or in a particular situation.

THE CHARISM OF THE HOLY SPIRIT

The last word is that the Holy Spirit is the true spiritual director and soul friend. Every Christian has received the Holy Spirit's anointing in conversion and baptism, and the experienced indwelling of the Spirit is the inheritance of every child of God.

The Spirit resides in the Church corporately and in every believer personally, and he is the advocate, interior guide and giver of gifts of wisdom and discernment.

It is my vocation as a Christian to keep my feet firmly planted within the Church catholic, with the Bible in my hand and the Holy Spirit in my heart. The voice of the Spirit will then sound within the Church's fellowship, within the text of Scripture and within my own interior life.

It is the work of the Spirit, then, through members of the body of Christ, to impart spiritual gifts and ministries, including spiritual direction and soul guidance. In this way, not only will the Church and the believer be built up in faith, but seeking people in the world will recognize the wisdom and compassion which ought to mark the community of Christ, and will seek soul friendship on their own path, and the network of love will spread.

Part III

PASTORAL
REFLECTIONS

Preparing
the veggie garden

17

The Bedrock of Scripture

THE DYNAMIC OF INSPIRATION

Throughout all my writings, as throughout all my life, Scripture has enthused, guided, judged and inspired me. It is not a dead letter or a legal document in which its authority is vested in some mechanical theory of inspiration, but it is rather a living witness, a joyful declaration, a message of salvation — a love letter from God himself.

In this chapter I do not want to lay down some dogma of inspiration that leads to a literal fundamental interpretation. Neither do I want to go to the opposite extreme and think that I can sit in judgment on the revelation of God in Scripture, treating it in a subjective and cavalier manner and, therefore, evading its central teaching. Rather, I want to communicate the canon of writings which have been recognized (not created) by the Church, and upon which my faith, life and eternal welfare rests, as the bedrock of authority. It is with joy and enthusiasm that I do this, for I continually respond to the life-giving revelation contained in the Bible as I read, sing and meditate upon the dynamic revelation of which it is said:

The word of God is living and active, sharper than any two-edged sword, piercing until it divides soul from spirit, joints from marrow; it is able to judge the thoughts and intentions of the heart.

(Hebrews 4:12)

The word *inspiration* is rare, for it only occurs once in the New Testament, but it is a powerful analogy, and its implications are found throughout the whole Bible. It occurs in 2 Timothy 3:16.

All scripture is inspired (theopneustos) by God and is useful for teaching, for reproof, for correction, and for training in right-eousness, so that everyone who belongs to God may be proficient, equipped for every good work.

If I were to translate literally, then the word *theopneustia* would be rendered 'God-breathed', and the reference is to God breathing into Adam's nostrils the breath of life so that he became a living being (Genesis 2:7). This breath of God is the Holy Spirit, for the Hebrew word *ruach* and the Greek word *pneuma* both mean spirit, wind or breath in the Old and New Testaments. This breath of God is universal, moving throughout creation, breathing life and fertility, sustaining animate life in all sentient beings and inspiring all that is creative, good and true in human endeavour. The same Spirit of God breathes in creation and redemption, opening the eyes of the sinner, communicating the powers of the new birth, and inspiring the human heart through the words of Scripture. Mary Lathbury's words illustrate it perfectly:

O send your Spirit, Lord
*   Now unto me,*
That he may touch my eyes
*   And make me see;*
Show me the truth concealed
*   Within your Word,*
And in your Book revealed,
*   I see you, Lord.*

Another important witness to Scripture is found in 2 Peter 1:21, which includes the apostolic warning that only the Holy Spirit who inspired Scripture can interpret it aright:

No prophecy of scripture is a matter of one's own interpretation,
because no prophecy ever came by human will, but moved by the
Holy Spirit, saints of God spoke from God.

The Greek verb rendered *moved* in this quotation literally means being *borne along*, just as the ship in which St Paul travels in Acts 27:15, 17 is borne along or driven (NRSV) by the wind. As a ship is borne along in the sea by the wind in its sails, so the prophet is borne along by the Holy Spirit in inspiration, so that the prophet delivers divine revelation and not simply a private opinion or interpretation.

The safeguard here is that the same Spirit who inspired Scripture must interpret it within the fellowship of the Church. This saves us, on the one hand, from the private presuppositions and prejudices of a contemporary commentator who subjects Scripture to the critical judgement of the passing age, and on the other from the exclusivist and heretical sects which abound today, with their private interpretations. Scripture is given within the community of the Church and must be interpreted within the same discipline. I do not mean that any one communion of Christ's Church holds a monopoly of the truth, but that the teaching of the historic Church down through the ages is the guardian of the deposit of faith (1 Timothy 6:20; 2 Timothy 1:14), and that the Holy Spirit, within the whole mystical Body of Christ interprets the Faith in every generation. The canon of catholicity respecting the fundamentals of the Faith concern *'quod semper, quod unique, quod ab omnibus'* — those things which have always and everywhere and of all have been believed, within the Church of God. The treasure house of Scripture is the source of inspiration, the constant rule of life and the touchstone of faith. It is the Holy Spirit who keeps such faith and interpretation alive within the Church. It is refreshing to read the preface to the foremost Catholic commentary on Scripture *The New Jerome Biblical Commentary*, where the Catholic scholars acknowledge the creative work done by Protestant scholars and on which they had to depend, within the awareness of the unifying work of the Holy Spirit. The words of St Augustine are relevant here:

In things essential, unity,
In things non-essential, liberty,
But in all things, charity.

THE SELF-AUTHENTICATING WORD

We do not, therefore, disregard scholarship in favour of some kind of mystical intuition of an esoteric kind. Such an attitude must be suspect in favour of disciplined and dedicated ecumenical scholarship through which the Holy Spirit can work in interpretation, reinterpretation and application in every age.

Scripture is not interpreted by private and biased cleverness, but in the light of the Spirit's work within the catholicity of the Church. We all have our pet foibles and doctrines, not always rooted in Scripture, and some of us would like to mould and alter the canon of Scripture to our own ends, whether we are Anglicans or Catholics, Pentecostals or Presbyterians, Baptists, Methodists or Quakers. We are all under the authority of Scripture within the fellowship of the wider Church.

Nevertheless, we must avoid a literalist, fundamentalist view of Scripture, for violence, bloodshed, holy wars and discriminations of every kind have been buttressed by Scripture texts, and it is salutary to note that nearly all the heretical sects affirm a plenary inspiration of Scripture, and at the same time deny the divinity of Christ, and therefore Incarnation and the Holy Trinity.

I am not arguing a blind submission to an infallible Church, nor to an infallible Bible, but to the self-authenticating word of God in Scripture. Calvin is often more biblical than those who followed him, and at the beginning of the *Institutes* he writes of the inner testimony of the Holy Spirit to the word of Scripture:

Those whom the Holy Spirit has inwardly taught truly rest upon Scripture, and that Scripture indeed is self-authenticated; hence it is not right to subject it to proof and reasoning. And the certainty it deserves with us, it attains by the testimony of the Spirit. For even if it wins reverence for itself by its own majesty, it seriously affects us only when it is sealed upon our hearts through the Spirit.

This matter of self-authentication is certainly part of my own experience of Scripture, both in personal devotional life, in public church and group ministry, and in the wider world of unbelievers with whom I have dialogued in enthusiastic and friendly dialectic. I feel I know from the inside a prophetic and apostolic feel for the voice of God.

The old prophets, like the apostles, were burdened with the word of God. Jeremiah cried out because the fire of God burned in his bones, and the Psalmist was aware of the searing flame of inspiration within him. Amos was not in the line of the prophets, nor had he any prophetic training, but God called him powerfully, and he makes it very clear: 'The lion has roared; who will not fear? The Lord God has spoken, who can but prophesy?' There was no choice. It was a holy burning, a divine compulsion, and if it brought loneliness, rejection and persecution, then so be it. Jeremiah spells it out:

> O Lord, you have enticed me, and I was enticed;
> you have overpowered me, and you have prevailed.
> I have become a laughing stock all day long; everyone
>   mocks me . . .
> For the word of the Lord has become for me
>   a reproach and derision all day long.
> If I say, 'I will not mention him, or speak any
>   more in his name,'
> then within me there is something like a burning fire
>   shut up in my bones,
> I am weary with holding it in, and I cannot.

Such self-authentication of the word of God is not in this case comforting, but fearful and overpowering. Throughout Scripture the analogies used for the word of God are all effective instruments for powerful truth. The word of God is a fire that burns, a hammer that strikes, a sword that cuts. It is manna that feeds, milk that sustains, and meat that strengthens. The Hebrew word *dabar* means not only a *word* but a *thing*, and when the *dabar-Yahweh*, the word of the Lord, goes from his mouth, it actually *does* something. It accomplishes God's will, and does not fail in its purpose.

The prophetic word is like an arrow, a spear, a sword, that pierces, cuts and wounds the hardened sinner and hypocrite, but heals and sustains the repentant sinner who is wounded by the divine Love.

In such dynamic experience lies the self-authenticating power of the word of God. It is a twofold inspiration of the Spirit. First there is the divine power by which the word is begotten in the mind and heart of the apostle and prophet — that is *objective* inspiration. Second there is the inward illumination which takes place in the enlightened mind and heart of the believer — that is *subjective* inspiration. Holy Scripture stands as the authoritative, written word, objectively inspired by the Holy Spirit, and the believer who is open to the interior illumination and subjective inspiration of the Spirit is the one who is led deeper into the life of meditation and prayer, with all its corporate, social implications.

THE LITURGICAL USE OF SCRIPTURE

There are many different ways of living the hermit life, and the amount of liturgical prayer and Scripture varies a great deal with different brothers and sisters. I need the solid structure of the daily office with its rhythm of Scripture, Psalms and reflection at morning, noon, evening and night. It is in Scripture that I find my spiritual food, I am given direction, I am built up in the faith. I cry out with joy, with pain, with complaint, assurance and glory as I repeat and sing the Psalms which reflect every mood from ecstasy to despair. It is certainly the case that people who have been incarcerated find that the Psalms minister to them at an existential depth that meets them, understands them and gives them a real voice in their deepest need.

I have called this chapter 'The Bedrock of Scripture' because I cannot do without a disciplined, progressive reading of, and meditation upon, Scripture every day of my life. Of course God is not limited to Scripture. He can and does speak in many other ways. It is true that the Church existed before the New Testament, indeed that the New Testament was born from the experiential heart of the Church. Nevertheless, the Church did not *create* the canon of Scripture, but *recognized* it. The complete canon of Scripture was the result of the long, praying deliberation of the Church, and it records and recreates the saving and healing experience of Christ wherever it is read and proclaimed in faith.

I do not want to impose the daily office as an additional duty upon the busy Christian, but it is necessary, not only to give attendance to the word and sacrament every Sunday, but also to ensure that there is a prayerful reading of Scripture every day, whatever form it takes.

I was brought up to believe that Scripture was at the heart of the reformed tradition and that there was a neglect of Scripture in the Catholic tradition. But my actual experience was that I did not receive any disciplined training of saying morning and evening prayer with its rich content of Scripture in the free church tradition, but as an Anglican priest, in theological training and parish experience, I found such a discipline already in place.

In these ecumenical days this is being remedied, for it is common for Baptists to be reciting the daily office and for Catholics to be participating in devotional Bible study, and often sharing these together in retreats, conferences and parishes.

Liturgical Psalms, canticles, readings, antiphons and hymns are either pure Scripture or derived from Scripture. Where this is not the case there must be a continual pruning and reforming of liturgical material so that it manifests a truly biblical and ecumenical theology. Scripture is at the heart of the celebration of the Eucharist, and it is now evident that there is a common liturgical basis to the eucharistic rites of all the main line churches, and a shared understanding between liturgical scholars on liturgical principles.

A great deal of experiential and textual liturgical work was done at Taizé from the 1960s, where there was a pooling of Reformed, Catholic and Orthodox liturgical thinking in the light of the Second Vatican Council. It must also be acknowledged that the charismatic movement in all the mainline churches has introduced and stimulated freedom and spontaneity in worship, so that both liturgical and charismatic elements may be woven into the fabric of satisfying and sustaining worship.

Far from it sounding odd that a hermit should be so

concerned about the common liturgical experiments and practices of ecumenical liturgists, it is essential to me in solitude
that I should be abreast not only of theological and devotional
thinking in the wider Church but that I should aim for liturgical
wholeness in my worship. I am not engaged in a platonic flight
'of the alone to the Alone', but a living, worshipping, praying
member of the Body of Christ, aware both of the communion
of saints in heaven and contributing to the thinking and practice of the Church on earth. And Scripture is the bedrock of
our faith and life.

THE DEVOTIONAL LOVE OF SCRIPTURE

This chapter has obviously not been concerned with a doctrinal
and theological treatment of inspiration and of the canonicity
of Scripture, and though I would have much to contribute in
these areas this is not that kind of book. What I have been
concerned with is the recognition and use of Scripture for
instruction, guidance and food on the journey – more a prag-
matic necessity than a doctrinaire position. When I say
'Scripture is inspired because it inspires', I realize that this is an
unsatisfactory doctrinal statement, but then, I am writing for
hungry beggars and not for professional dieticians!

But I am not satisfied with a simple devotion to the Bible in
a naive sense, for I continue to keep abreast of contemporary
biblical criticism. I have observed extreme pendulum swings
and am intrigued to trace the change of fortunes in the reputation of that creative scholar, my old enemy, Rudolf Bultmann!
I am not anxious to get my reader embroiled in such a tangled

area, but I would advise a perusal of the excellent articles on inspiration, canonicity, biblical criticism and hermeneutics (interpretation) in the *Jerome* commentary I referred to earlier.*

So it is not as an intellectual discipline of study that I speak of Scripture here, but as a pastoral guide, a sustaining food, and a warming and blazing fire in your bones. As Jerome himself said: 'Love the holy Scriptures, and wisdom will love you. Love wisdom and she will keep you safe. Honour wisdom, and she will embrace you.' Jerome was wise enough to know that there is no objective knowledge of Christ other than through a devotional love of Scripture, for in spite of many decades of critical study, and many thousands of printed pages, there is no way to any 'historical Jesus' other than recourse to the source material of the New Testament which is the witness of the early Church. The New Testament is a book of proclamation and devotion more akin to a Gospel tract than an objective biography, but that very element of witness, experience and evangelistic fervour is the Spirit's work and inspiration told out in the apostolic preaching and writings.

Let me illustrate the devotional use of Scripture from my own life. Last week a retreatant came to talk over his own prayer journey with me, after which we knelt together in my chapel hut before the Vladimir icon, and recited from memory Psalm 131. The words which held us still before the Lord were a wonderful picture of the contemplative feeding upon the word of God:

* Raymond E. Brown, *The New Jerome Biblical Commentary*, (London: Geoffrey Chapman, 1993). The pb. Student Edition is much less expensive than the hb.

I still my soul and make it quiet,
  like a child upon its mother's breast;
my soul is quieted within me.

He and I make a practice of learning passages of Scripture which we store in mind and heart, so that we can meditate, ruminate, 'chew the cud' throughout the day. He has also acquainted himself with the Greek text of the New Testament (though a layman), and this is a great devotional help not only in Bible study but in using verses in Greek as material for meditation and repetition. Every morning the first audible words of prayer that I speak are those of Galatians 4:6 in Greek: 'God has sent the Spirit of his Son into our hearts, crying, "Abba, Father!"' Because of their daily repetition, these words, like the Greek version of the *Jesus prayer*, have become second nature to me, and increasingly precious as revelation and experience of God.

THE WORD OF GOD

This chapter stands under the section 'Pastoral Reflections' because I am vitally concerned with the matter of where Scripture figures on your list of priorities. It is no good developing a life of prayer, or working your way through any other parts of this book if you neglect the devotional study of Scripture.

I may be critical of Christians who have no disciplined life of meditative prayer, but I am equally critical of those who spend much time in reading books and dabbling with techniques of meditation while they neglect the study of the Bible. It is essential that your spirituality is grounded in the Word of God. There is no Christian spirituality without a firm basis in Scripture. What do I mean here by 'the Word of God'?

Karl Barth reminds us that the *Word of God* meets us in a threefold form. First there is the *Living Word* which is Jesus Christ himself, who is the fullness of God's revelation. Then there is the *written word*, the Bible, which is the witness to the Living Word. And finally there is the *proclaimed word*, which is the life-giving voice of the Church in its preaching, teaching and living the very life of Christ in the world.

It is Christ himself who constitutes the source and fullness of this unity, and it is the Holy Spirit who is the bond of union. He transforms the dead letter into the living spirit (2 Corinthians 3:6), which is what we mean by interior inspiration, and he indwells and energizes the Church in the preaching of the Gospel so that men and women are born into the kingdom of God through such anointed proclamation.

That is why we can speak of the sacrament of the word as well as the sacrament of the Eucharist, for it is the same life-giving Spirit who is at work in each of them. The living voice of God speaks in the reading and exposition of Scripture in the marketplace, in the believing community and in the meditative cell where Scripture has primary place.

Where the Bible is honoured in reading, exposition and devotion, there the Holy Spirit is at work, actually accomplishing the will of God, objectively transfiguring the believer and transforming situations. The prophetic words of Isaiah 55:10f. make this very point:

As the rain and the snow come down from heaven, and do not
return there until they have watered the earth, making it bring
forth and sprout, giving seed to the sower and bread to the eater,
so shall my word be that goes out from my mouth; it shall not
return to me empty, but it shall accomplish that which I purpose,
and succeed in the thing for which I sent it.

In concluding this chapter I want to look at St Luke 24:13–end.
During the Emmaus walk the two disconsolate disciples were
overtaken by the hidden Christ – hidden by their lack of perception. During their conversation he listened sympathetically
to all their words of pain and loss, and then began to expound
the prophetic Scriptures, causing such a conflagration of hope
and joy in them that they said of the experience afterwards:
'Were not our hearts burning within us while he was talking to
us on the road, while he was opening the Scriptures to us?'

As they were describing this encounter to the disciples in the
upper room, suddenly Jesus himself appeared among them. They
became agitated and terrified, thinking they were seeing a ghost.
But Jesus calmed their anxieties with his words of peace. He
showed them his wounded hands and feet, and assured them by
eating fish and honey in their presence. Then occur the wonderful
words which bear witness to the prophetic power of Scripture,
and continue as the sustaining source of our spiritual life:

'These are my words that I spoke to you while I was still with
you – that everything written about me in the law of Moses, the
prophets and the psalms must be fulfilled.' Then he opened their
minds to understand the scriptures.

18

Prayer, Study and Manual Work

ALL HUMAN LIFE IS THERE

I remember when the above words were first used in an advertising slogan to promote a Sunday newspaper which contained (and still does!) all sorts of seedy stories reflecting the very real, though partial, elements of our society. I believe the reporting of such stories panders to the worse voyeuristic instincts of the public, but the idea behind the slogan was that it was all 'very human' as if pigs at the trough was an apt analogy of our humanity. I must add that pigs at a trough, in itself, is a very beautiful picture, and from the pigs' point of view, a very satisfactory one!

I mean to redeem the image of being human – especially in the light of men and women who are made in the image of God. This means that human beings have a vocation to be humane, and therefore more human. I also want to affirm that our humanity has elements which are physical, mental and spiritual, and to split off these areas into tight compartments does not make for an integrated and unified life. The reason why so many contemporary people are restless and world-weary is because they lack the vital spiritual element in their lives. And the reason why so many religious people lack vitality and integration is because their understanding of God and the spiritual life is somehow confined to the religious realm. Their God belongs to the holy place, the holy day, the holy category, and the remainder of life is lived without the awareness of the vital, divine mystery which suffuses the whole of our humanity.

My spiritual pilgrimage, traced at the beginning of this book, was grounded in the simple but mysterious fact of myself in relation to the natural order in my childhood. The later understanding of the evangelical and Catholic dimensions of faith over a period of years, enabled me to achieve a closer approximation of the integrated unity of faith and life. By the time I reached the hermit symposium at St David's in 1975, all the ingredients were there, all the elements were in place in my thinking, but it was only when I began to experiment with prayer in solitude that I got it all together in experience.

Isn't this a strange claim to make – that it was a simple hermit lifestyle that enabled me to experience my humanity at a previously unknown level? I must admit, though, that I had joyfully, sorrowfully and freely mingled in many-dimensional relationships with all kinds of people before I took off into the desert. I do now have letters (and visits) from people who are impatient and restless to try a hermit life, and it is sometimes transparently clear to me that they are people who are running away either from the world or from themselves – perhaps both. It is a paradox that you need a certain maturity to attempt this life, and that maturity is increased as you live it. Thomas Merton writes of the spectres of greed, futility, boredom and madness which face contemporary marketplace men and women, and then says this about the basic simplicity of the hermit life:

The hermit is, or should be, happy without having a happiness machine to solve his problems for him. He faces boredom squarely with no other resources than those he has within himself — his own capacities and God's grace. He puts these resources to work, and discovers that his life is never boring. On the contrary, renouncing care and concern about getting somewhere and having fun, he finds that to live is to be happy, once one knows what it is to live in simplicity.

This matter of integration is important because it not only indicates, for me, the growing experience of getting the compartments of my spiritual, mental and physical life into some kind of harmonious unity, but is a clue to the underlying need for a psychological maturity which brings together the disparate elements of my temperament.

This does not mean a quiescent, vegetable existence, but a creative, working tension in which interior balance and reciprocal relationships flow from a unitary source of life and love which is at the heart of simply being human. The reason I'm being 'up front' about this is not because a hermit should live his or her life in public (mostly they don't!), but because part of my vocation is communicating through my writings the wholeness of my life to the reader, sharing the sorrows and joys so that life may be seen from the vantage point of living mostly in solitude. And this has a great deal to say to both the harassed, hyperactive person, and the bored, unemployed person in our marketplace society. So let me take up the elements of our threefold theme.

THE THREE ELEMENTS OF MY LIFE

I want to show how these elements contribute towards a unified understanding of what I am about, and perhaps it will be easier to start 'from below' without implying that there is anything demeaning about manual work. In fact, I often find that the sense of God's creative presence breaks into manual work in surprising ways, as if the Lord 'plays a game' with me as a lover creeps up upon the beloved in welcome surprise.

MANUAL WORK

There are all the basic things which need to be done, like keeping myself clean, washing clothes, preparing and cooking food and maintaining the huts, enclosure and surroundings without mod. cons. Living alone does make me realize how cleanliness and orderliness indicate a positive and healthy attitude of mind. Fortunately, I do like inventive cooking, and with no meat I need to give attention to a balanced diet, while the baking of bread is always a joy.

Apart from domestic tasks I enjoy the creative work of bookbinding. Last month I repaired and refurbished a beautiful English Missal for a church in Ipswich, and this week I have had two teaching sessions, instructing a novice in bookbinding. I also like mounting many different kinds of icon reproductions for sale through my outlets, and though I wish I had received a proper training in carpentry, I do manage to make prayer stools and bookstands.

None of this work is physically hard, so I need the vegetable garden to work up a good sweat. Just now I am doing the autumn digging and manuring, and this morning I received a gift of 100 daffodil bulbs, and I've just dug up a giant leek, a kohlrabi and some spinach towards the meal I shall be cooking after writing this chapter.

During this last season I grew the following in our veggie garden: broad beans, runner and French beans, leeks, cabbages, beetroot, carrots, swedes, parsnips, turnips, spinach, kohlrabi, lettuces, onions, courgettes and outdoor tomatoes. Mostly the harvest was excellent, though the caterpillars took advantage of my non-spraying attitude!

Quite apart from theologizing on the cycle of seasons, and the times of being bowled over by the loving surprise of God's mysterious presence, I am humbled and overjoyed in the actual physical work and its outcome in a basic vegetable garden. It is an immense satisfaction to grow food for the monastery and to be able, like today, to simply go into the garden and pick vegetables for my dinner. The physical effort, cold and muddy days, the demanding and consistent labour involved, is all of a piece with my spirituality of being simply human.

The desert fathers (and mothers) found that manual work was not merely desirable but absolutely necessary to their spirituality, and the Bible teaches that the Holy Spirit is not only manifest in the natural order and cycle of seasons, but that artisans are actually inspired and imbued by the Spirit in their physical work and designs (Exodus 31:1–11). It was not by accident that Jesus was a carpenter (Mark 6:3). The years at Nazareth certainly sanctified manual work.

THE HEART OF PRAYER

STUDY

My home was a loving and joyful place, but it was not an academic atmosphere, and the only books were cowboy stories for my father and romantic novels for my mother. So I worked haphazardly through our local library, devouring indiscriminately all that appealed to me until, at twelve years, I was given some systematic help in my local church. Indeed, I owe to my local church and my religious quest the stimulation of my curious mind. I was overwhelmed, when preparing to enter theological college, to discover the various disciplines which were needed for theological competence. They included philosophy, languages, history, sociology, anthropology, psychology, plus all the biblical and religious elements of pastoral training. My theological education took me to Cardiff, Zurich and Edinburgh, and I'm still at it! – and shall be till I die – and then it will begin in earnest.

Because I repair monastic library books I keep abreast of many disciplines, (our library is a thematic rag-bag), and dip into an *Introduction* to various worlds, filling in the wide gaps in my knowledge and enabling me to respect the areas of intellectual, scientific and artistic study, while I paddle in shallower pools.

I keep up my Greek by following the New Testament lessons in the Greek text before Compline each night, but my intention to revise my biblical Hebrew remains in the area of good resolutions. My primary training was in systematic theology, and I keep up my reading in this area, and in the growing interfaith studies in spirituality. I am kept alert and open to dynamic growth by the words of St Augustine:

*Further let me ask of my reader, wherever alike with myself he is
certain, there to go on with me; wherever alike with myself, he
hesitates, there to join with me in enquiring; wherever he recognizes himself to be in error, there to return to me; wherever he
recognizes me to be so, there to call me back. (De Trinitate I,5).*

I am grateful for the undergraduate and graduate worlds of
which I have shared part, and encourage the reader as part of
his or her human journey and spiritual life, to integrate intellectual study with the physical and mental dimensions of existence. One of the CMS prayers which should undergird your
intellectual life runs as follows:

> From the cowardice that dare not face new truth,
> From the laziness that is content with half truth,
> From the arrogance that thinks it knows all truth,
> > Good Lord, deliver me.

PRAYER

St Francis was somewhat suspicious of study because he knew
some of the pitfalls of older monastic life, and saw the same
intellectual élitism and conceit arising among his own friars,
together with the owning of small libraries giving the literate
friar power over the simpler brothers.

I say this under the heading of 'prayer' because I have
observed in my three countries of theological study the way in
which intellectual élitism gets in the way of true theological
study, and also how certain kinds of biblical criticism militate

against a true understanding of biblical truth.

There are two kinds of people especially that I have noted – those post-graduate students who, because of lack of prayer, or slothful familiarity with Scripture or theology have lost vision and enthusiasm; and those professional critics who import their unbelieving preconceptions to bear upon the text so that they stand in judgment of Scripture and never allow Scripture to judge them.

I stand in the wider Franciscan tradition (shared with many others) of living under the authority of Scripture, of openness to solid biblical criticism and diverse theological interpretation, while at the same time keeping understanding with the mind and intuition of the heart together in creative interpenetration. I know that sentence takes some unpacking, but read it over and sort out the diverse and important elements.

I would find it very difficult to live without books and without the stimulus of a wide diversity of theological opinion. I delight in broad horizons, and I must confess that I enjoy reading those with whom I strongly disagree! But I am aware that many in the desert tradition entered into solitude and prayer without books or intellectual learning, and in this way penetrated more deeply into the mystery of God. I began this desert part of my vocation indicating my willingness to let go the writing of books, and I realize that I may be called upon to let them go entirely at some time ahead.

The form and content of the life of prayer is dealt with in other parts of this book, but here I am emphasizing the need to keep together those elements of my human life which are so easily compartmentalized. The presence and reality of God is mediated through body, mind and spirit, and fellowship with

Christ must be a daily experience of sharing with him in work, study and prayer, so that the sap of the Holy Spirit will rise in my human spirit as it rises in the plants and trees of my garden in the spring.

A THREEFOLD CORD

This threefold cord will not easily be broken (Ecclesiastes 4:12), and if body, mind and spirit are dedicated in a unity of purpose and daily discipline, then if one fails I will be sustained by the other two.

If my body falls sick then the reservoir of my mind and spirit will give refreshment toward healing and strength to bear the affliction. If my mind fails then my spirit and body will move in the channels of habit and disciplines long learned, and if my spirit seems to find itself in a dry and thirsty land, then the diligent continuance in physical and mental disciplines will keep me in patience until God visits me again with the refreshing dew of his Spirit.

The Waters of Dick Brook

19

When The Spring Dries Up

LOSS OF VISION

I remember my reaction when going up to Edinburgh to pursue some exciting postgraduate theological study, meeting a few dog-eared students who having been working at their Ph.D. theses for three years or so, had lost their vision along the way. The reasons were diverse: a bad supervisor who had communicated academic boredom; a worried reduction of the scope of their area of study until it had lost its life and creativity; a sedentary life of study with no exercise or spontaneity; a scintillating social life which left no time or energy for anything else. Whatever the reason, the vision was lost, and with that, the accompanying loss of warmth and vitality about present study and future possibilities.

This experience made me measure up my own life with its wide spectrum of interests and activities, its priorities and spontaneities, lest I should tread the same path, for there is nothing worse than meeting a man or woman who was once alive and sparkling, now down at heel and melancholy.

This also happens in the spiritual life, in every part of the Church and within the diversities of spiritual teaching. It is made much more difficult for the fundamentalist Catholics, evangelicals or charismatics who feel they must maintain their glow, keep their end up, and not let the party line down. Covering up a loss of joy or vision with a voluble and projected pretence is a miserable existence and the sure way to anxiety, depression and sickness. Much better to be open, honest, sharing, and to find a good soul friend in whom to confide, because you are not always the best judge of what is *really* going on in your mental or spiritual life.

TWO EXAMPLES

For instance, take Martin, who had experienced a sudden and dramatic conversion experience at his university Christian union as an undergraduate, and who entered enthusiastically into his new life of dedicated fellowship, Bible study, team evangelism and missions, with the enjoyment of new and vibrant friends. There was the excitement of a whole new spiritual dimension opening up where before there was listlessness and a restless drifting from one relationship to another.

After leaving university and finding a lively church in his new area things went well for a year or so, and then he began to neglect his prayer life, to lose interest in Bible study, to miss the intensity of the university Christian group with its constant and satisfying demands upon the group and the individuals within it. One day in church, Psalm 51 was being sung, and he let the words wash right over him:

Create in me a clean heart, O God,
and put a new and right spirit within me.

172

Do not cast me away from your presence,
  and do not take your holy Spirit from me.
Restore to me the joy of your salvation,
  and sustain me with a willing spirit.

He closed his eyes, and sighed for a vision lost, an enthusiasm waning, and an excitement abated.

Or take Fiona, in her mid-twenties. She and her partner James had attended the Sacred Heart Church since they were children, and they had drifted together. She was a cradle Catholic and had kept up her church duties, confession, regular attendance at Mass, but it was all very pedestrian and conventional – rather dreary if she was honest.

Then one evening, a friend at work had invited her along to a convent in the next parish where there was an ecumenical charismatic group. It was not the sort of thing her own parish went in for, and she was a bit cautious, but Freda persuaded her, and she went along.

The meeting was not held in the convent chapel, but she felt assured by the atmosphere, for these were the sisters who had nursed her mother some years previously. There were about thirty people present, mostly Catholics, but a sprinkling of other Christians too, though you wouldn't know it unless you were told.

After the welcome and mutual greetings there was an informal start to the proceedings with a few contemporary hymns and Taizé chants, accompanied by a small group with guitars and wind instruments. Fiona found herself quite enjoying the new experience. There followed a brief prayer of invocation, and a Bible study on 1 Corinthians 12:1–12, dealing with the charismatic gifts of the Holy Spirit in the body of Christ, led by the parish priest. This gave way to open discussion in which anyone was free to participate. This was strange to Fiona, but even more strange was the time of open worship and prayer which followed, for although it began with some traditional prayers, it soon became extempore. Freda began quietly singing in 'tongues' and the whole group joined in. Fiona felt a prickly sensation of unease, and yet it was strangely beautiful – almost like the chanting of some Orthodox monks she had heard on Classic FM.

This went on for about twenty minutes, and then the priest asked if there were any who needed the laying on of hands for healing or any particular problem that needed to be prayed for. Four or five people responded, and a small group of men and women laid hands on them and prayed after a brief exchange with each one, while the rest of the meeting surrounded them with a quiet hum of prayer, intercessions and singing. So many things seemed to be going on at the same time, but there was no confusion or disharmony. It all seemed to flow into a traditional hymn, with the prayer: 'The Lord bless you and keep you . . .' to conclude. No one was in a hurry to leave, and though it had mostly been strange to Fiona, she felt held in a warm embrace of friendship and acceptance which was new and welcome to her.

All that had taken place two years previously, and Fiona began to attend the meetings regularly. After about four meetings, she entered into an experience of the Holy Spirit in which she had found herself caught up in a prayer of praise which gave way to what she had learned was the gift of tongues. This was accompanied by a tremendous inflow of joy and awe, and the whole experience overflowed into her parish life at home.

The celebration of the Eucharist became alive to her, the study of Scripture was a new delight, and the whole dimension of the spiritual life was seen, for the first time, as an adventure, a pilgrimage, and a real heartfelt experience of grace.

James was not at all keen at first, but he strung along, and though keeping it at arm's length, he was not averse to the lively liturgy and informal musical Masses that were sometimes part of the scene.

Fiona found that this new dimension shed its light on the whole of her life. She looked at her personal lifestyle, her relationship with James, and her social awareness, which was practically nil, and she found herself getting involved with the Catholic aid project CAFOD, and Amnesty International. It deepened her commitment to the Catholic Church, and she enjoyed fellowship and discussion with other Christians, realizing how much more concerned they were with true unity than were some members of her own parish.

All this was wonderful, and she learned to face obstacles, temptations and changes of mood with the grace which God gave her, and with the sustaining strength of the sacrament and group fellowship. She felt herself disappointed with the practice of confession, for now she had new areas to explore and many questions to ask. Her confessor did not seem to understand the questions, let alone give her direction, but she determined not to transfer her allegiance to the neighbouring parish where the traditional liturgy and charismatic manifestations seemed to blend together harmoniously.

It was into the third year that she found areas of her spiritual life drying up. First of all there was difficulty in meditating on portions of Scripture, and the use of imagination in applying the Bible to her situation. Then there was less ability to pray verbally or to use the gift of tongues in private prayer, and this had formerly been a great delight to her. She also found herself strangely empty and restless during the meetings of the group, and even using her discernment in a critical way when she felt that people were too emotional in their worship, or liked the sound of their own voices in group Bible study.

She was thrown into confusion, for increasingly she lost the joy of fellowship; private Bible reading seemed not to be relevant to her life or the needs of the world, and even the sacrament became again a matter of duty. She found herself depressed and sometimes irritable when people questioned her, and yet she did not find joy in any other interests; indeed music and drama, which had always provided immense satisfaction, now also lost their power. She was miserable with God and miserable without him.

PERPLEXITY AND CONFUSION

These are two examples of the spring of religious experience and joy drying up. We do not know enough about either Martin's or Fiona's lives to be able to diagnose the real reasons for the loss of vision and sensory enjoyment of God. Could it be secret, unconfessed sins, compromise of moral principles, wrong relationships, neglect of prayer or a spirit of creeping lukewarmness? Or is there another set of possible reasons? Certainly God seems to have withdrawn the sense of his loving presence, there is a certain darkness and aridity in religion, and an increasing reluctance and inability to pray.

I think of some of my friends who have known such experiences, and certainly sometimes there has been a real neglect of the spiritual life, a compromise of ideals, an eye to ambition, preferment, or a materialism which has choked up the spring of grace. Loss of moral integrity or the sudden or gradual involvement in doubtful relationships has brought spiritual catastrophe in its wake, and sheer physical and mental exhaustion has dried up the spontaneous spring of joy in some lives.

But there are some who have come to me with a sense of aridity, emptiness, and loss of spiritual vitality, who deep in their hearts are concerned, worried and anxious lest they have themselves caused such spiritual darkness, and who mourn over the loss of God's loving presence.

Some of them have kept up an outward attendance at worship and even strenuously pepped up the time and energy they give to the social commitments of their faith. The priests and pastors have had to keep 'performing' the celebration of the liturgy and the preaching of the word, with all the pastoral demands which are part of professional ministry. This makes it even worse for them. You can see how the continuance of such deprivation can lead to depression, melancholy, anger or even despair.

It becomes not only more difficult but extremely hurtful when they receive contradictory advice. On one side they are counselled that a loss of vision and joy must be the result of unconfessed and unforsaken sin with backsliding, so they must repent and beseech God to renew and visit them again. On another side they are told to keep on striving in prayer, put more energy into working at it, act out joy and rejoicing in a charismatic group until it starts flowing again.

All such advice may be completely astray, and it is no wonder that the great masters of prayer like St Teresa of Avila or St John of the Cross complain about bad spiritual direction:

Some spiritual directors are likely to be a hindrance and harm rather than a help to these souls that journey on this road. Such directors have neither enlightenment nor experience of these ways. They are like the builders of the tower of Babel. When these builders were supposed to provide the proper materials for the project, they brought entirely different supplies, because they failed to understand the language. And thus nothing was accomplished. Hence, it is arduous and difficult for a soul in these periods of the spiritual life when it cannot understand itself or find anyone else who understands it.

(St John of the Cross, *The Ascent of Mount Carmel*,
Prologue 4).

Whatever the reason, the spring has dried up, and there is confusion and perplexity over the reason for it. This is not only a matter of the spiritual life, for we are one whole being. The mental life is affected by lassitude and accidie, and physical wellbeing has given way to listless tiredness and loss of energy. Life itself has lost its savour, and nothing lends a sense of enhancement and excitement to existence.

We have come to the end of a chapter with such a situation. What are the reasons, what is the diagnosis, is there a discerning understanding and a possible prescription for such a dis-case? Let us turn to such possibilities.

20

Depression or The Dark Night of the Soul?

THE GIFT OF DISCERNMENT

We were left in the last chapter with a basic problem of discernment. Where is God in all the perplexity and confusion of my arid and empty life? Am I sinful? Am I depressed? Am I simply exhausted? Or is the Holy Spirit at work somewhere, reducing me to a state of helplessness and dependence, so that I am thrown on to his grace alone?

A brother (who had a tendency to melancholy and simple glumness), came to me one day and said: 'Ramon, do you think I am experiencing the dark night of the soul?' I looked at him with the suggestion of a smile, and replied: 'No B——, I think you probably ate too much cheese for supper last night.' The ploy worked and he was soon chuckling over the big deal he was making of the basic personal temperamental difficulty he had to come to terms with. The problem was a gift of discernment and he needed help not only to diagnose the situation, but to see the way forward.

The gift of discernment of spirits (*diakrisis pneumaton*) is a Gospel charism (1 Corinthians 12:10), and much was made of it in the desert tradition and among the mystical teachers of prayer. It means the identification of the presence or absence of

God in human circumstances, especially in the changing moods and evolving awareness of our spiritual lives.

Another encouragement to discernment is found in 1 John 4:1: 'Beloved, do not believe every spirit, but test the spirits to see whether they are from God.' There is a testing, sifting, judging, discerning of the human spirit in all its affective movements, and there is also a similar judgment awareness in relation to the spirit of true and false doctrines and practices in the Church and the world. We cannot do it alone, we have the anointing of the Holy Spirit to teach us (1 John 2:26), and within the body of Christ there are those with gifts of discernment to enable you to come to a right evaluation of what is taking place in your interior life.

Of course it is possible that if you feel a certain emptiness, aridity, bored listlessness, loss of vision and energy, with periods of depression, it may well have causes for which you are responsible and which need to be put right. As to depression, well if it is serious, clinical depression, you will need trained and professional counsel and treatment, but that should be clear in the symptoms that present themselves. This chapter is not dealing with that clear medical category.

It may well be that your symptoms are part of a psychical make-up indicating a temperament which you must learn to recognize, embrace and live with. For instance, if you find you are one of those people who suffer from *Seasonal Affective Disorder* (SAD), you will find that there is a 'light' treatment which may afford you immense relief, but you will also learn to recognize that when the darker months begin in late autumn you will have to cope with a certain darkening of your moods with a promise of welcome light at the end of the tunnel when spring appears.

It may also be possible that you have underestimated the workload you can carry, or the stress that you can bear at home, university, work or even in your wider relationships. Physical exhaustion dragged Elijah down to a fit of suicidal depression, and he needed tender angelic ministry and nourishment to set him on his feet again (1 Kings 19:3–9).

Your spiritual problems may also have a physical basis in disease, alcohol or chemical dependence, or even lack of exercise. You must learn to know yourself, to be in touch with your body, to be at ease with your whole being, for you are a psychosomatic unity. All this is an encouragement for you to get in touch with your whole self, to be open and real with yourself about your attitudes and habits, and to have a relationship of integrity and honesty with a soul friend with whom you can share all your fears, hopes and aspirations.

THE DARK NIGHT OF THE SOUL

There is another explanation of why a person who has known and loved God in Christ over a number of years, and has rejoiced in sacramental gifts and graces may find the life of meditative and intercessory prayer drying up, a loss of vision and enthusiasm for evangelistic and pastoral ministry, and a withdrawal and absence of the sense of God's loving, guiding and joyful presence.

It becomes difficult, and even dangerous, if these people are fully committed Catholics or evangelicals, or professional priests or pastors, for the temptation then will be to keep up a zealous, smiling, Catholic or evangelical front, in spite of desolation, and arid emptiness within. This can lead to real depression, hidden anger and despair.

I have already referred to the harm done by sincere but mistaken and insensitive directors, urging the penitent to repent of hidden wickedness, to pray harder, do better and strive more valiantly. These are Job's comforters, lacking the discernment that it is God who is causing these symptoms in the soul. It is a divine withdrawal of the *sense* (though not the reality) of his loving presence, a divine drying up of the 'sensible' springs of emotional enjoyment of prayer and Scripture. God himself is taking away the joys of meditation and prayer in order that he might lead the soul into a certain darkness so that a new life of contemplation may begin to take root. If this is so, then the believer must not fight and strive, must not zealously apply worked-up energies to pray harder, make more sincere confessions or rush to the penitent seat hoping for emotional repentance. As St John of the Cross says again:

> The director does not understand that now perhaps is not the time for such activity. Indeed, it is a period for leaving these persons alone in the purgation God is working in them, a time to give comfort and encouragement that they may desire to endure this suffering as long as God wills, for until then, no remedy — whatever the soul does, or the confessor says — is adequate.
>
> (*The Ascent of Mount Carmel*, Prologue 5).

St Jane de Chantal manifests exactly the right attitude:

> O my Lord, I am in a dry land, all dried up and cracked by the violence of the north wind and the cold; But as you see, I ask for

nothing more; You will send me both dew and warmth when it
pleases you.

What, then, is this? St John of the Cross indicates that it may
well be the beginning of the Dark Night of the Soul. In his
beautiful poem *The Dark Night*, he portrays in eight stanzas the
path of the soul through the dark night of *sense* and *spirit*,
guided by interior illumination, to the vision of the divine
Lover and union with him in prayer and love.

This dark night begins to operate in those who have already
shown loving devotion to God, sometimes over many years of
discipleship and service, and who have known many special
gifts and graces both sacramental and charismatic, and are now
being prepared for the deeper life of prayer leading to divine
union.

It is a hard and demanding path, trodden by faith alone, and
where only the action of God is of any avail. The soul's task is
to 'let it be', to passively co-operate with the interior grace
that is at work in the believer's life, weaning the soul from the
senses and into the contemplative realm of the spirit. That is
why there is a twofold division of the *Dark Night* into the night
of the *senses* and the night of the *spirit*. The classic statement of
St John is found in *The Dark Night*, II. 5,1:

> *This dark night is an inflow of God into the soul, which purges it*
> *of its habitual ignorances and imperfections, natural and spiri-*
> *tual, and which the contemplatives call infused contemplation or*
> *mystical theology. Through this contemplation, God teaches the*
> *soul secretly and instructs it in the perfection of love without its*
> *doing anything or understanding how this happens.*

> *Insofar as infused contemplation is loving wisdom of God, it*
> *produces two principal effects in the soul: it prepares the soul for*
> *union with God through love by both purging and illumining it.*
> *Hence the same loving wisdom that purges and illumines the*
> *blessed spirits, purges and illumines the soul here on earth.*

You would imagine that this 'inflow of God into the soul' would produce radiant joy, ecstasies of wonder, trembling of body, mind and spirit in the sheer adoration of the power and love that must enlarge and illumine the receiving soul. But no! This is a *dark night*, says John, and it is dark because the dazzling radiance of God has this effect upon the soul which is beyond the soul's comprehension, and searing to the soul's weakness and impurity. He puts it this way:

> *Why, if it is a divine light (for it illumines and purges a person of*
> *his ignorances), does the soul call it a dark night? In answer to this*
> *there are two reasons why this divine wisdom is not only night and*
> *darkness for the soul, but also affliction and torment. First, because*
> *of the height of the divine wisdom which exceeds the capacity of the*
> *soul. Second, because of the soul's baseness and impurity; and on*
> *this account it is painful, afflictive, and also dark for the soul.*
>
> (*The Dark Night*, II. 5,2).

What John is saying here is that the soul is separated from God by the chasm of *Being*, and the chasm of *Holiness*, and that when God enters the soul which is both mortal and sinful, such trembling and purgation takes place; it results in darkness, pain and suffering, reducing the soul to helplessness, so that only God can complete what he has begun in the soul's sanctification.

TWOFOLD DARKNESS

This Dark Night is twofold. There is the night of the *senses* and the night of the *spirit*. The first takes place in the kind of person we have already described, one who has lived a life of devotion, with gifts and graces of the Spirit, and years of loving service to God. And this night of the *senses* is a work of God in which he weans the soul from a sensual, emotional and 'carnal' love, into a contemplative life of the *spirit*, in which love for God is lived by his grace alone, and is on an altogether higher plane.

But the way from carnal to spiritual love is purgation and suffering, for what must take place is a burning up of the dross of sin, carnality, and lesser love — a movement from the *senses* to the *spirit*, in which God does the work and the soul simply 'lets it be'. This results in a saintly life of grace, abounding in compassion, warmth, radiance and a reflection of God's image in the soul, and this makes the person more human and loving.

This is as far as I shall go in this chapter or even in this book, for St John of the Cross says that very few undergo the night of the *spirit* in this life, for that experience is so fearful, and the outcome so transfiguring that it is beyond words to describe, and that is why St John himself breaks off in description of such divine union — the ineffable is entrusted to his poetry.

The profound night of the *spirit*, if it happens in those rare souls on earth, begins after a long period of living the saintly life beyond the night of the *senses*. This is far beyond the present scope of our life of prayer. In any case it is not for us to seek experiences, but to seek God alone, and if he calls and moves us, then we can allow ourselves to be lovingly led by him, assured that he will bring us safely through the suffering and pain that is necessary. I cannot help but believe, after much meditation upon the life of St Francis of Assisi, that he is one of those rare souls who glimpsed, gazed, and entered into the searing love of God, even on this side of eternity.

THE SOUL'S RESPONSE

Therefore, if we confine ourselves to the night of the *senses*, this will be more than enough, for it means that men and women who are tasting the beginnings of this experience will already have disciplined their lives of prayer, and probably spent a fair time in helping others along the way. At this time they will encounter that strange aridity and dryness as the springs of felt joy and meditation dry up, and will become perplexed and confused as to what is happening to them, and turn to a trusted spiritual director to help them diagnose this condition.

St John of the Cross treats of this condition and its true diagnoses in three brief chapters* which are among the most important in his whole works. I wonder if they may apply to you? You have known a real love for God, Scripture has been your constant guide, the sacraments and worship are integrated into your spiritual life. You may be a priest or pastor, perhaps a sister who regularly conducts retreats and schools of prayer, or a friar who leads missions and loves preaching. You may have rejoiced in spiritual gifts and spent years of service for God in some sphere, or you may feel yourself to be an

* *The Dark Night*, I, chapters 8–10.

ordinary but devout lay person. But in any case, you have learned to let go your own will so that God can have his way, and you have overcome many temptations and obstacles, including negotiating periods of darkness and loss, and learned to understand your own temperamental swings of mood.

But now comes this new episode of almost continual and complete dryness. God seems absent, despite a desire to feel his love, and even though your head believes you must continue to trust him in hard and dark times, you feel he may have abandoned you and you are miserable.

I am suggesting to you that you are nearer God in your darkness than ever you have been in your whole life. That you are, in fact, on the edge of a new discovery of his love and grace, but there is a dark night of suffering to undergo in the process of being weaned from the life of the senses to the life of the spirit. God's contemplative light is darkness to you because of your mortality, your weak eyes and your carnal love. Because God shines *directly* into your soul, you are blinded, and it causes suffering. The shining of God is not now mediated through emotional sense experience, but via a new way of the spirit, and it is painful. The weaning from senses to spirit is hard to understand, and only if you let go of all striving and simply allow God to work within you will you come to see what is happening.

I used to be scared of deep water, and if I found myself just out of my depth at sea I would struggle and flail around in a combination of breast and overarm stroke until I could feel the firm sand beneath my feet again. I learned eventually that it was better to lie on my back, float freely and effect some rhythmic back strokes. So in this situation, when God is at work, simply float, be still, gentle, quiet, passive – let him do what he wants. Then you will find that this attitude itself, becomes a pattern of prayer.

Over the last five years, in my early meditation period, the best times have not been prayers of petition and formal meditation, but simply being – trusting, waiting, passive and still in the darkness. Not 'praying with my brains' but letting God *be*, allowing him to have his way in my interior life. This may sound new and different to you, but it is the way to transformation – and only God can do that.

So when a brother or sister comes to me with such symptoms of dryness, sadness, inability to pray, meditate or delight in God's presence – even feeling abandoned and forsaken by God, and having lost the vision and feeling of all the emotional delights that had accompanied prayer and dedicated service, I look for the cause.

Is it some known or hidden sin and compromise? Is it a particular bout of mood swing or depression based in present stress, anxieties, external worries or even low blood-sugar? I enquire about mental and physical health, exercise and lifestyle. If all these areas do not yield the reason, then I look for the possibility of oppression by dark powers attacking a weak point when the soul is unsuspecting.

As we go on, perhaps in a few sessions, and hold it all in quiet prayer before God, it becomes clear that my brother or sister, despite the feeling of dryness and abandonment, really *wants* to love God, is miserable because of the feeling of desolation, and is concerned about the things of God. Then I am able to say that he or she is in for the introduction to the new life in the spirit, and explain that there is a price to pay in this being weaned from the senses to the new and spiritual level. There is no need to worry over the emotional loss of carnal feelings that were once so satisfying. If Scripture, meditation and devotions have lost their attraction, they will return eventually at a new level, but just now God is leading another way. Listen to St John again, referring to the souls in this dark night:

> The attitude necessary in the night of sense is to pay no attention to discursive meditation, since this is not the time for it. They should allow the soul to remain in rest and quietude, even though it may seem very obvious to them that they are doing nothing and wasting time, and even though they think this disinclination to think about anything is due to their laxity. Through patience and perseverence in prayer, they will be doing a great deal without activity on their part . . . They must be content with a loving and peaceful attentiveness to God, and live without the concern, without the effort, and without the desire to taste or feel Him.
>
> (*The Dark Night*, I. 10,4).

WHERE AM I?

If we have gone thus far together – the brother or sister and I, they may then ask 'Where am I?' or indeed may ask me about this whole scheme of prayer: 'Where are *you*?' I want to respond by saying: 'I don't know, and it doesn't matter.' If we keep pulling up the plant to see if its roots are growing, it will be counterproductive.

I do know that I have encountered some strange and new

areas of contemplative prayer in the last decade or so, and that St John of the Cross has been an illuminating and perceptive commentary on so much of it. But I don't know whether I have known much or little of the classic scheme. In any case, we are all different and God doesn't schematize his dealings with us, though it is sometimes helpful for us to note the steps, methods, ladders, mansions, grades and categories of prayer which the great teachers have set down for our guidance.

But I do know that there have been times of aridity and absence which have nevertheless indicated from within that I must be quiet and silent. Indeed, between my two experimental periods of solitude and asking for permission to test it thoroughly, I was very aware of the interior words: 'Be silent or I will silence you.' And I *had* to obey – and I have found a prayer of silence and solitude which seems to me to reach beyond charisms, tongues, joyful singing, meditative delights and schematic praying, though all these have their place and I sometimes return to them.

It seems to me that it is all being integrated into a new wholeness, and I do know that there is a fearful darkness and wonderful presence on ahead that I have only glimpsed and dreamed about so far.

We are all on the road of prayer and love, so don't let this chapter disturb or trouble you. Let it be a chapter which may show you some meaning if the symptoms described in it occur in your life. St John tells us not to worry if we seem to be in a place of darkness and unknowing, and all our clever ways of preaching and praying are being lost to us. Perhaps we are being prepared for something deeper, truer and purer. We must simply let it be, and let him do it:

Accordingly, these people should not mind if the operation of their faculties are being lost to them; they ought to desire rather that this be done quickly so that they may be no obstacle to the operation of the infused contemplation which God is bestowing, that they may receive it with more peaceful plenitude and make room in their spirit for the enkindling and burning of the love that this dark and secret contemplation bears and communicates to the soul. For contemplation is nothing else than a secret and peaceful and loving inflow of God which, if not hampered, fires the soul in the spirit of love . . .

(*The Dark Night*, I. 10,6).

21

Nurturing a Cosmic Dimension

THE UNIVERSAL PRESENCE

Over the last decade or so there has been a distressing and needless separation of two poles of basic Christian teaching – creation and redemption. I understand in my head what the fears and priorities of both sides are about, but I don't understand in my heart. Indeed the root of the problem may be that the fears on either side are generated in the mind, and both sides need to pay more attention to the wholeness of the biblical witness, and the actual experience underlying both poles.

Stated briefly, the problem is that between 'creation-centred spirituality' and 'redemption-centred spirituality'. The first argues that the world is good from the hand of God and should be affirmed joyfully. People should not major on original sin, be obsessed by guilt or make the bleeding, agonizing Jesus the centre of their teaching, for this leads to a denial of natural and human joys and a negative attitude to all things creative, including all the aesthetic and celebratory aspects of human life, especially sexuality. There is an emphasis on God as creative artist, on the necessity of self-esteem and of creation as the play of God and the essential goodness of mother earth.

Here are some representative accusations made by the 'creative-centred' side against the 'fall-redemption' side: they tend to hate not only their sins but themselves as sinners; they major on penance and self-punishment, then project guilt on to others in judgemental attitudes; they hold negative images of God, continually needing to appease the masculine, judgemental aspects, so that God's love is conditional upon moral uprightness. Therefore repentance, confession and forgiveness becomes a repetitious treadmill, instead of a liberating act of creativity. Even when some writers try to hold creation-redemption in healthy tension, what they say can sound doctrinally suspicious from the other side. Take this paragraph from an orthodox Roman Catholic priest who is influenced by creation-centred spirituality:

> *This (creative) joy is missing from so many hearts. But there is more than joy in the face of our ever-creating Mother God, eternally birthing what is new and beautiful. There is delight and passion too. It was sacred passion that led to creation in the first place so that the intimacy of incarnation could happen later in time but first in intention. It was the burning passion of a God that assumed the vulnerability of a baby and experienced the ecstasy and the agony of an extraordinarily ordinary human being. It is with this passion that we, in turn, are graced as co-creators with God in loving our universe forward into a garden of Eden where fear and death are forever forgotten.**

I know that many of my 'redemption-fall' friends would

* Daniel J. O'Leary, *Windows of Wonder: A Spirituality of Self-Esteem*, (Dublin: The Columba Press, 1991), p. 89.

immediately smell out incipient heresies in that statement with its feminist orientation, its sexual imagery, its lack of sin-redemption awareness, and its Pelagian implications – and they have a case.

This brings us to the complaints of the 'redemption-centred' side. They argue that the world is not good, but fallen, tainted, dark and cruel, and that humankind is not naturally good but sinful, selfish, twisted, perverted and violent. They maintain the holiness of God who demands justice and atonement for sin, and that only repentance and forgiveness through the redeeming work of Christ upon the cross, and the new birth through radical repentance and faith in the finished work of Christ, can lead human beings into a life of righteousness and truth.

They point out that to use the language of liberty, creativity and sexual affirmation without an experience of salvation and a life of discipline is to lay oneself open to libertarianism and hedonism. Images of God which stress femininity led to sexual irregularities in Canaanite religion, and that is why the Judaeo-Christian tradition maintained masculine language and imagery.

TRUTH IN CREATIVE TENSION

The creative and redemptive aspects of spirituality must mingle in holistic harmony, for redemption is the reconciling of a broken creation, and positive creativity is the consequence of the healing and reconciling power of redemption.

If you emphasize creation to the detriment of redemption, the result may be a sentimental theology which does not take seriously the exceeding sinfulness of sin. If the patient is suffering from a pernicious terminal sickness, calling for radical surgery, an extra dose of vitamin supplement will not bring healing.

Creation spirituality has also drawn to itself all manner of 'new age' barnacles which embrace spiritism and syncretistic cults, practising esoteric fertility rites employing erotic language which tends to the abuse and not the affirmation of wholesome sexuality.

On the other hand, if redemption is emphasized to the detriment of creation, then the Church becomes obsessed with the fall in the book of Genesis, instead of affirming the clear priority of the innocence and goodness of the created order as it came from the hand of God. This leads to such dark doctrines of sin as the total depravity of humankind and an *absolute* rupture between God and his creation in which the divine image is not only broken, defaced or damaged (which it is) but utterly destroyed, allowing no continuity or relation at all between God and the people he has created. Thus, suspicion is cast on all human endeavour, so that sexuality and creativity are suspect at root level, and creation is so fallen that it cannot reflect anything of the divine presence or love. Humankind becomes *massa perditionis*, a universal mass or lump of damnation; and it has even been taught that racial sin is propagated from parent to child in the physical act of generation.

I find myself saddened by the polarization of these positions. Spirituality is both creation and redemption centred. If you think back to my childhood experience in the introduction, you will see why I want to affirm a creation-centred spirituality. Biblically, innocence preceded guilt, the goodness of creation came before the fall. And I find that when I share my faith I want, first of all, to affirm common humanity, compassion, yearning, and I want to point to human restlessness as the evidence for God's image in us, longing for wholeness and love.

It would be foolish to be so naive as to deny that something terrible has happened to the goodness of creation, or to ignore the brokenness of the image of God within us. That is where the amazing divine love meets with us. God himself became incarnate, as one of us, entering into our darkness, bearing our sin, our guilt, our sicknesses and pain. He became incarnate in order that he might show us the divine compassion in a true human being, and in that life exemplify forgiveness, healing and joy. Then he laid down his life in sacrifice, shedding his blood for our redemption, and rose in power as the Saviour of humankind, calling us to follow that trail of glory. This means being born into his kingdom of love by repentance, faith and forgiveness, to share hereafter in the eternal kingdom of heaven.

If we can hold together the biblical witness of creation and redemption, then we shall find the solution to the problem of our restlessness and yearning, and shall enter into the evangelical experience of salvation from our sinful past and go on to affirm all the creation blessings of paradise restored as children of the new creation.

My evangelical experience, even at twelve years of age, enabled me to embrace Christ as Saviour, Friend and Brother, and this redemptive understanding was rooted into the good soil of a nature-mysticism in which the reality of God's loving presence was known by intuition and felt in the natural order.

Grace builds on nature, and the liberating experience of the blessing of the Holy Spirit at sixteen years of age, enabled me to affirm the goodness and wonder of the created order of nature and humankind, in spite of the fact that sin and evil had invaded our poor and wonderful world. The more I was able to affirm God in all things (apart from sin), the more I could claim them for him as a child of light, love and truth, so that I may enter into my redemptive inheritance and bring the whole world to his feet.

It is possible to read the following verses with guilt, and fear of judgment. But it is also possible to read them in affirmation of the divine presence irradiating the universe with divine glory:

> Where can I go from your Spirit?
>   Or where can I flee from your presence?
> If I ascend to heaven, you are there;
>   if I make my bed in Sheol, you are there.
> If I take the wings of the morning
>   and settle at the furthest limits of the sea,
> even there your hand shall lead me,
>   and your right hand shall hold me fast.
>
> (Psalm 139:7–10)

The whole Psalm is saturated with wonder, awe, praise and adoration of the God who indwells the heart of creation, and it is this same God who became incarnate in Christ, who indwells the believer by his Spirit, and whose redeeming love will one day be consummated in the transfiguration of the whole cosmos in glory.

CHILD OF NATURE AND OF GRACE

My evangelical experience did not deny my nature mysticism; indeed they belonged together. I have had problems with opposed theological systems in the Church, but their resolution has taken place in a meditative and contemplative return to my childhood experience. I therefore consider myself a child of nature and of grace, and my understanding of the Gospel impels me to share the good news of forgiveness with fellow sinners, and to live a life of rejoicing and compassion in the world.

This is easy to state, but it means becoming involved with the healing of the world's wounds in human sympathy, international peace and justice, and ecological awareness. It would take volumes to unpack these three areas of concern, and this book has been involved with the spiritual foundation from which such concerns arise. But let me quote two writers who clearly and succinctly present a theology (*orthodoxy*) and a discipleship (*orthopraxis*) which indicate the divine-in-human pattern of my spirituality. The first comes from the seventh century St Isaac of Nineveh (Iraq), one of the greatest Orthodox spiritual writers, who influenced the Russian novelist Dostoevsky:

> *An elder was once asked, 'What is a compassionate heart?' He replied:*
>
> *'It is a heart on fire for the whole of creation, for humanity, for the birds, for the animals, for demons and for all that exists. At the recollection and at the sight of them such a person's eyes overflow with tears owing to the vehemence of the compassion which grips his heart; as a result of his deep mercy his heart*

shrinks and cannot bear to hear or look on an injury or the slightest suffering of anything in creation.

'This is why he constantly offers up prayer full of tears, even for the irrational animals and for the enemies of truth, even for those who harm him, so that they may be protected and find mercy.

He even prays for the reptiles as a result of the great compassion which is poured out beyond measure — after the likeness of God — in his heart.'

If you take this kind of experiential, orthodox spirituality, and translate it into the new awareness and concerns of our own time, we become concerned with our own unprecedented, sinful destruction and desecration of our world. Thomas Berry writes of the interdependent network of the divine and human balance in the cosmos in the 1989 edition of *The Catholic Worker*:

We should be clear about what happens when we destroy the living forms of this planet. The first consequence is that we destroy modes of Divine presence. If we have a wonderful sense of the Divine, it is because we live amid such awesome magnificence. If we have refinement of emotion and sensitivity, it is because of the delicacy, the fragrance, and indescribable beauty of soul and of music and of rhythmic movement in the world about us. If we grow in our life vigour, it is because the earthly community challenges us, forces us to struggle to survive, but in the end, reveals itself as a benign providence. But however benign, it must provide that absorptive drama of existence whereby we can experience the thrill of being alive in a fascinating and unending sequence of adventures.

In both these writers, over 1100 years apart, ancient and modern, eastern and western, there is that sense of our humanity woven into the fabric of the whole cosmic order. From such a vision of holistic spirituality there emerges an overwhelming intuition and practice of compassion. It is a vision which realizes the anguish and pain of our existential situation displaying human and cosmic brokenness. But it does not despair, for in that same situation there co-exists a profound sense of awe, wonder, order, beauty and pattern. These are the two dimensions which call forth the yearning and experience of redemption, and which stimulate the quest for beauty, design and order in individual and cosmic existence.

The revelation of God is Trinitarian, and the wonderful pattern of my own life is a reflection of that objective revelation in the created order — both in the story of redemption and in the universal breathing of the Holy Spirit.

As I pray and study in the ecumenical atmosphere of the Church, despite our schismatic separations, I find that threefold awareness shared among the men and women of prayer and theological concern. It has to do with the mystery of the divine presence which I know by intuition and responded to in my childhood; with the specific evangelical experience which laid hold on me at twelve years of age, gently introducing me into the catholicity of the undivided Church; it has to do with the immersion into the Holy Spirit at sixteen years, which set my feet firmly on the way to relating the threefold experience to the whole of humanity.

I want to share the inwardness of my present hermit vocation with you as you read, for whatever our lifestyle in the world, it is our task to encounter the presence of God just where he has placed us, and to relate our interior life to the context of daily existence. Here, in my enclosure, I feel the wholeness of the desert tradition, and continue to explore the contemplative tradition which God has revived in the Church. There is also a refreshing new exposure to the eastern tradition greatly enhanced by the growing Orthodox presence in the west. When a new book by the Orthodox writer Olivier Clément entitled *The Roots of Christian Mysticism** was published, I found an immediate response to the pattern in which he links brilliantly selected texts from the early eastern teachers with profound, and often mystical, exposition.

His aim is to reach back to the spiritual theology of the undivided Church, revealing both its biblical rootedness and its relevance to contemporary thinking concerning our relationship with the created order in the context of a cosmic revelation. It is quite clear that he is caught up in a mystical spirituality which is creation- and redemption-centred, opening up the ancient and contemporary quest for wholeness and holiness in the contemplative life. And such a life is the basic inheritance of every human being, for without it they are lost and empty of necessary spirituality.

GETTING IT TOGETHER

If the consequence of deepening your life of prayer is to drive you into some exclusive or spiritual ghetto, pursuing your own esoteric vision which does not involve you in spiritual and

*London: New City, 1993.

practical work for the healing of our world, then your spirituality is a sham. It is a pretence which will being you to eventual disintegration, and will be shown, on the Day of Judgement, to be the hypocritical mask it really is.

The closer a man or woman follows the contemplative path, the closer he or she is to the concerns of such societies as *Pax Christi*, *Amnesty International*, the *Campaign Against the Arms Trade*, or other of the positive healing agencies of compassion in our world. If you join a contemplative group, make sure it has a compassionate outreach to the world's need, or join yourself also to a helping agency.

Obviously, you can't do everything, and limits must be drawn in terms of your individual and your group's outreach. It would be stupid to become frenetically active because of some contemplative vision which you have glimpsed, for that would subject you to compassion fatigue. If you are a 'young married' then as a mother or father your primary contemplative duty is the praying, playing and working with your own children and spouse. And if your own children enable you to become childlike again, this will prove to be a basic and immediate way of relating to the world.

Nurturing a cosmic dimension began for me in childhood, and I believe this ought to be the basis upon which a life of joy and compassion is built. Unfortunately, many children are denied such a birthright, and others have the primal vision 'educated' out of them. The loss can be made up in later life though it is difficult, and the more we enable people to learn ways of contemplative prayer and to develop an open receptiveness to each other and to the created order, the closer they will be to God's intention for his people.

In conclusion let me illustrate such openness in quoting from a personal letter from his friend Kathleen, to Daniel O'Leary, speaking of a childhood contemplative moment which gave orientation to the whole of life:

> *We walked together in the field. I can never forget the spot where it happened. I was barefoot on the green grass. My Dad was beside me. It seemed like he was totally present to me and to all of nature. I remember feeling that his love, just then, was unconditional. And then something happened. It seemed like I connected with the trees, the wild flowers, the stones, the birds, the whole universe, my Dad and my own heart. A moment stood still in time. It was so powerful. That moment has stayed with me ever since. I became a child of nature. I connected with everything in the cosmos.* *

This is not a piece of sentimentalized fiction, but the recalling of a creative cosmic moment in the childhood of someone who grew up with it, held it in mind and heart, and allowed its reality to colour every part of her growing and adult life. That moment of cosmic awareness gave primacy to loving relationships, to personal integration, and I recognize it as a parallel to my own experience. Such awareness and immediacy is to be nurtured as a divine gift, and shared to your enjoyment and God's glory.

---

* Daniel J. O'Leary, *Windows of Wonder*, pp. 41f.

Epilogue

LET'S GO ON TOGETHER

If you've worked through this book, putting into practice some of the counsel and methods commended in it, then you've been on a strange journey into areas where most people never venture.

It is quite clear that radical assumptions have been made — that there is a God who loves his creation, who providentially leads his children into the joy and sorrow of human loving in order that they might become more human and more Godlike.

You will have seen that I believe that every human being is meant to nourish a contemplative dimension in his or her life — indeed that we were created for contemplation. This is the basis of our life and love together in the world, and those who neglect it do so at their spiritual peril. It is, therefore, a prerequisite for that fuller life in God when our earthly pilgrimage is over.

I have shared enough of my own life here to stimulate your life of prayer. I do not encourage people to become hermits, but to live an ordinary life of reciprocal love in the world. But I am here for you in order to pray *for* you in the context of the Church and the world, and in order to pray *with* you to help you take up the offered disciplines of the spiritual life as they speak to your condition.

You and I are members of the Body of Christ, and our vocations may have carried us in different directions, but we belong together. Some of the people who come to see me live most busy and demanding lives, and if they did not develop a contemplative oasis in the midst of it they would go under. Different members of the body have different functions and ministries, and that is how it should be. But all of us must learn to pray, to love, to share, and to reflect more and more the glory, the enthusiasm and the compassion of the God who calls us into an ever deepening and intimate fellowship with himself.

Let's go on together then, and continue to share the discipline and spontaneity of these chapters. Our lives mingle in contemplation and action, and the heart of prayer is the rhythmic beat that pulses through the whole of creation. And that heartbeat is the Holy Spirit.

Appendix

FURTHER INFORMATION

1 Anglican Renewal Ministries, 6 Scriven Road, Knaresborough, North Yorkshire, HG5 9EQ.

2 Retreats: There are many books on retreat with the addresses of retreat houses, but there is only one organization and magazine that is vital. The National Retreat Association (NRA) was formed in 1989 and it includes retreat groups from Anglican, Baptist, Methodist, United Reformed, Roman Catholic and Quaker traditions. Its annual magazine *Vision* includes not only excellent articles and book reviews on all matters to do with the wider dimensions of spirituality, but the addresses of all retreat venues in Britain and Ireland, and information about or announcements of retreats for the coming year. The NRA address is: 24 South Audley Street, London W1Y 5DL.

3 The Christian Meditation Centre: 29 Campden Hill Road, London W8 7DX.